1837 — 1887.

Hawaiian Mission Children's Society.

JUBILEE CELEBRATION

—OF THE—

ARRIVAL

—OF THE—

MISSIONARY REINFORCEMENT OF 1837.

Held April 9th, 10th and 11th, 1887.

HONOLULU, H. I.
DAILY BULLETIN STEAM PRINT.
1887.

Windham Press is committed to bringing the lost cultural heritage of ages past into the 21st century through high-quality reproductions of original, classic printed works at affordable prices.

This book has been carefully crafted to utilize the original images of antique books rather than error-prone OCR text. This also preserves the work of the original typesetters of these classics, unknown craftsmen who laid out the text, often by hand, of each and every page you will read. Their subtle art involving judgment and interaction with the text is in many ways superior and more human than the mechanical methods utilized today, and gave each book a unique, hand-crafted feel in its text that connected the reader organically to the art of bindery and book-making.

We think these benefits are worth the occasional imperfection resulting from the age of these books at the time of scanning, and their vintage feel provides a connection to the past that goes beyond the mere words of the text.

As bibliophiles, we are always seeking perfection in our work, so please notify us of any errors in this book by emailing us at corrections@windhampress.com. Our team is motivated to correct errors quickly so future customers are better served. Our mission is to raise the bar of quality for reprinted works by a focus on detail and quality over mass production.

To peruse our catalog of carefully curated classic works, please visit our online store at www.windhampress.com.

HISTORY OF THE CELEBRATION.

At the Board meeting of the Society held at the residence of P. C. Jones, Esq., Oct. 9, 1886, the President called attention to the fact that April 10, 1887, was the fiftieth anniversary of the landing at these Islands of the reinforcement of 1837, consisting of thirty-two missionaries, the largest company ever sent out by the A. B. C. F. M. to any of its missions, and suggested that it would be a fitting thing for the Cousins' Society to celebrate this event. The proposition was cordially endorsed by all, and recommendations to that effect were submitted to the Society, which as heartily adopted them, appointing the Board of Managers a committee to carry out the same.

As it was ascertained that the regular meeting of the Society would come upon Saturday evening, April 9th, the following plan for the Jubilee celebration was adopted. This meeting constituted the first session of the Jubilee, and was held in the large dining-room at Kawaiahao Seminary which had been beautifully decorated and adorned for the occasion. In lovely evergreen upon the wall facing the audience was the motto: "1837—Mary Frazier—1887." And most happy was the date, for the "Mary Frazier" had really made harbor that day, 1837, and anchored outside for the night.

On Sabbath evening, April 10th, a union service of the Bethel Union and Fort-St. Churches was held, conducted by Rev. C. M. Hyde, D. D., assisted by Rev. J. W. Smith of Koloa, and Mr. Edward Bailey of Wailuku, at which time Rev. W. B. Oleson preached the sermon.

On Monday, April 11th, two sessions were held on the grounds of Oahu College at Punahou. The first at two P. M., in a large lanai erected on the lawn for the purpose; the second in the parlors of the College at seven P. M. At these meetings were read papers especially prepared for the occasion by the survivors of the Mission of the A. B. C. F. M. to these Islands. These papers are printed in full. Between these sessions the ladies served a substantial lunch, and the time was spent in social intercourse. The attendance at all these meetings was large and the deep interest manifested showed how firm a hold these themes have upon our Society and the public also.

In December, the following circular letter was sent to all the survivors of the Mission. It is reprinted here to explain the personal and biographical character of the papers:

HONOLULU, H. I., Dec. 20, 1886.
To the Fathers and Mothers of the Mission of the A. B. C. F. M., to the Hawaiian Islands.

LOVED AND HONORED PARENTS:

We, your children and grandchildren of the Hawaiian Mission Children's Society send you greeting:— We rejoice and thank God that so many of you have been spared to see the near approach of the fiftieth anniversary of the landing on these Islands of the reinforcement of 1837. We desire, at that anniversary, to celebrate the Jubilee of their arrival. We propose to gather as many of you as we can, all if possible, at Honolulu, about April 10, 1887, and, upon that day and the 11th, to celebrate in religious and social gatherings this remarkable and historic event.

Therefore we invite you to join us on that occasion, asking that you be our guests, allowing us to bear all the expenses of your visit and to care for you as long as you can remain in Honolulu.

It has been thought advisable to have commemorative religious services upon Sunday the 10th. We also desire that these meetings shall be made memorable by the contribution, on the part of the survivors, of such papers as they can prepare, containing reminiscences of the work and history of the Mission. Especially do we request that you will speak freely of your personal experiences and work; and we venture to suggest that the Mothers of the Mission whose husbands have entered upon the rewards of the eternal life, make their papers largely biographical, describing the life and work of their husbands and themselves. We would especially entreat you to be with us, and hope that this gathering may aid in still further promoting the work of Christ here in these Islands and furthering the cause of Missions generally. Will you please favor us with an early reply to this letter, as we need to know your purposes, both as to attendance and what you can contribute to the commemorative services.

On behalf of the Board of Managers,

W. C. MERRITT, President.

At the gathering at Punahou the following survivors of the Mission were in attendance: Mr. and Mrs. Edward Bailey and Mrs. M. A. Alexander, from Maui; Rev. J. W. Smith, Mrs. M. S. Rice and Mrs. M. J. Rowell, from Kauai; Rev. Lowell Smith, Mrs. J. M. Cooke, Mrs. Lois S. Johnson, Hon. S. N. Castle, Mrs. S. N. Castle, Mrs. U. S. Emerson, Mrs. J. M. Damon, Mrs. L. B. Coan,

Rev. S. E. Bishop, and Rev. A. O. Forbes, from Oahu.

At the close of the evening session it was ordered, by vote of the Society, that the papers prepared for this Jubilee be published. The committee would call especial attention to the valuable statistical tables prepared by Hon. S. N. Castle.

---o---

MINUTES OF THE MEETING HELD AT KAWAIAHAO SEMINARY, APRIL 9, 1887.

The meeting opened in the usual manner with singing followed by a prayer from Mr. E. Bailey.

The President Rev. W. C. Merritt in the chair.

The minutes of the Board and also those of the previous meeting were read and approved.

The musical entertainment consisted of a piano solo by Mrs. Hanford, entitled "The Norwegian Wedding Procession," and a vocal duet by Prof. Van Slyke and Mr. Levi Lyman, entitled "Larboard Watch."

There were four papers from the Maile Wreath Committee. The first by Mrs. Merritt, "A Greeting to Our Missionary Guests;" the second by Miss Payson, "Medical Science in China;" the third by Rev. W. B. Oleson, "The Resumption of the Missionary Work among the Hawaiians;" the fourth by Mr. W. O. Smith, "The American Board and the Hawaiian Mission."

After the reading of the Maile, the President read a telegram received from Rev. Judson Smith, sending greetings to the Jubilee Celebration of April 10th, from the A. B. C. F. M.

The corresponding secretary, Mrs. L. B. Coan, then read letters from Gen. S. C. Armstrong, Rev. Oliver P. Emerson and Dr. G. Pearson.

Rev. W. B. Oleson then read the resolutions drawn up by the committee appointed at the previous meeting.

It was voted that the resolutions be adopted and a copy be sent to the Prudential Committee of the A. B. C. F. M.

Rev. S. E. Bishop, by request, read the resolutions adopted by the Hawaiian Board to be sent to the American Board.

The request was made that a copy of the paper read by Rev. W. B. Oleson, for the Maile be sent to accompany the resolutions as a paper prepared especially for the Society.

The President asked for a few remarks from Hon. S. N. Castle, Mr. E. Bailey and Dr. J. W. Smith, who were present.

The name of Rev. Hans Isenberg was recommended and he was duly made eligible for membership.

The collection amounted to $42.40.

There were about 120 persons present including the "Veranda Brigade."

The Society adjourned to meet again on Monday at Punahou.

Respectfully submitted,
W. J. FORBES, Rec. Secretary.

REPORT OF COMMITTEE, APRIL 9, 1887.

The Hawaiian Mission Children's Society assembled on the fiftieth anniversary of the arrival at the Hawaiian Islands of the largest reinforcement of missionaries, representing as such Society does the descendants of missionaries and such others as have allied themselves with them through kindred purposes and sympathies, do respectfully submit the following memorial to the Prudential Committee of the American Board of Commissioners for Foreign Missions.

WHEREAS, Unforeseen changes in social and industrial conditions have greatly modified the means and methods of Christian work among Hawaiians, and in consequence of these changes, Hawaiian Churches are greatly enfeebled, and the Hawaiian ministry find themselves unable unaided to meet the present emergency; and

WHEREAS, The deplorable loss to the the Hawaiian Ministry and Churches of the wise counsel, sympathy and presence, of missionary fathers is well nigh irremediable; and

WHEREAS, These Hawaiian Churches must constitute the nucleus about which Christian effort and influence must center in the religious future of these Islands; and

WHEREAS, We are firmly convinced that a judicious reinforcement of religious work among Hawaiians on the part of the parent society would greatly alter the condition and outlook of Hawaiian Christianity; and

WHEREAS, Those in these Islands who are able and disposed to aid in the support of Christian work are already, in proportion to their means, contributing largely to such work, and with the many demands upon them feel unable to assume and guarantee the support of new missionaries, and in view of the fact that in addition to the funds necessary for the support of such missionaries, considerable amounts will be required to be provided here for matters incidental to their labors; therefore be it

Resolved, That the American Board of Commissioners for Foreign Missions be requested to commission not less than five choice Christian men, as soon as practicable, for such work, and assume their support; such men to engage in such branches of work and at such centers or points as shall seem feasible and wise to the Hawaiian Board.

W. C. MERRITT,
WM. B. OLESON, } *Committee.*
W. O. SMITH,

---o---

THE RESUMPTION OF MISSIONARY EFFORT AMONG HAWAIIANS.

BY REV. W. B. OLESON.

It is an open secret that the American Board is to be asked to supplement its former work on these Islands by definitely resuming missionary operations. The conviction has ripened that the burden of the financial responsibility for the maintenance of religious effort among Hawaiians should not fall primarily on the Christian public

here ; that owing to the peculiar constitution of
the Hawaiian Board, it is inexpedient for it to
officially assume the responsible direction of new
agencies ; that the Christian public in the United
States ought to assume an intelligent and responsible share in the furtherance of fresh effort
among Hawaiians ; and that the experiment initiated in 1863, having essentially failed in its
purpose, the only feasible and adequate remedy
for the present condition of affairs is for the parent Society to resume its work where it left off.
When the American Board formally withdrew
from further missionary operations here, it was
with the conviction that " the Protestant religious community of these Islands" was competent
to wisely administer with occasional aid "all the
departments of Christian charity and Gospel
effort." It was expected that "all the needed
missionaries" would be found "among the missionary children—among the children of the foreign Christian residents, and among the native
Christians." It was felt that this responsibility
"for the building up of Christ's Kingdom within
itself" was "just what this community needed for
its own healthful and vigorous intellectual, moral,
and social development (p. 401, The Hawaiian Islands, by Dr. Anderson). It was not then known
what a strain would be placed on this Island community outside of this most important work. It
was not then known that this little community
would be called upon to provide for a large and
shifting population of Godless Anglo-Saxons
drawn hither by our industrial development ; or

that it would need to initiate and sustain unaided a work among the Chinese resident here, the mere mention of which would oppress with dismay a compact, and prosperous Christian community in the home-land with twenty times the resources and population of our Christian community.

And yet Dr. Anderson certainly had a sort of presience of our present dilemma here; for he wrote twenty years ago, "nor should we look on quietly, and see the Churches that have been planted at so much expense of money and labor, and with so many prayers and tears, fall a prey to invaders. A conquest that cost so much is worth a costly effort to sustain it; and who can doubt that, should there be a call for such an effort, it will be made?" p. 402.

The retrograde movement has set in, and has already gathered a tremendous momentum toward irreligion and heathenism. And at no time have Christian forces at the Islands been so sadly in a minority as at present. The call for renewed evangelistic effort is so clear and urgent, and the responsibility of the American Board in the premises is so undoubted and definite, that nothing, other than an extreme conservatism on the part of its Prudential Committee can much longer delay a truly just and equitable course toward the work here.

The responsibility of the American Board to sustain missionary operations among the natives of these Islands is unquestionably greater than the obligations to provide Protestant privileges for such Catholic Christian lands as Austria and Spain. There is a far more strenuous obligation te preserve the results of Protestant endeavor here than to maintain Protestant institutions and agencies in lands that are overwhelmingly Christian.

The responsibility of the American Board to resume missionary operations here is unquestionably greater than the obligation to enter new fields with the Gospel message. It is not contracting our sympathy for those who are living without Gospel light for us to urge the necessities of the population here. The American Board is not the only missionary organization, and it does not carry all the burden of the world's evangelization. No other Society could properly enter this field, and undertake the work that needs to be done ; whereas it is eminently fitting that the American Board having initiated missionary operations here should sustain them until the Island community is amply able to meet the obligation itself. No organization has any moral right to vacate its lasting obligation to nurture the spiritual life it has brought into existence. No organization has any moral right to enter a land with Gospel agencies except it be with the consecrated purpose to abide in that land till the end of time, if need be.

The responsibility of the American Board in this matter is directly to the race which it dislodged from heathenism and bore into the light and liberty of a Christian civilization; and indirectly to the vast constituency of missionary organizations the world around, who have gathered stimulus from the phenomenal triumphs of the Gospel here, and who ought not to be subjected to the needless disheartenment and dismay of a possible collapse of Protestant Missionary effort among the Hawaiian people.

Let not foreign Christians resident on the Islands abate one whit of their personal responsibility in affording a proper reinforcement to the religious work among Hawaiians. Let us rather add emphasis to the increased demands that should be made on our Island resources of money and service for the truly urgent necessity that is upon us in the present emergency. But while we do this let us bear well in mind two fundamental facts, viz., that it is essentially unjust to put the financial and official responsibility for new work among Hawaiians on the small Christian community resident here that are in sympathy with the work of the American Board; and that it is very essential that the whole truth as to the present condition of the Hawaiian people should be frankly reported to the constituency of the American Board in order that they may properly understand their responsibility in the premises. To all intents and purposes this community occupies a relation to the American Board similar to that of other communities supporting the Board's work. There is no reason in the nature of things why the Board should assign responsibilities to this community that it does not undertake to assign to other communities elsewhere.

I make a plea to-night for a little more liberty

in this matter of accepting responsibilities. I believe that this community is ready to generously contribute both in means and service to the American Board in case it definitely resumes missionary operations here. But I do insist that the full content of responsibility for this work be clearly understood. It lies heavily on resident Christians. Perhaps—I think very likely, we do not realize how great our share is. But it lies heavily on the constituency of the American Board in the home land, and I am sure that constituency is in only the slightest degree awake to its responsibility.

It never will be aroused to its responsibility until it is conversant with the situation and is formally pledged to sustain anew the work of American missions in this field.

It is high time for the heavily burdened Christian community here to make a dignified stand in asserting, along with a confession of its own obligation the lasting responsibility of the American Board not semi-officially through its Prudential Committee, nor sympathetically through a few Churches and individuals but unitedly through the voice and prayer and gifts of its whole constituency to strengthen the things that remain in the religious life of this people. This Jubilee anniversary of the arrival here of the largest missionary reinforcement sent to these Islands offers a suggestive opportunity for calling public attention to the urgent needs of our Island work; and in no wiser or more appreciative way can we honor the labors of the brave men and women who wrought so well here by the grace of God than by making the call loud and definite for other men and women of like spirit to labor among the same people to-day.

SERMON.

BY REV. W. B. OLESON.

I Kings, VIII:57.—The Lord our God be with us, as He was with our fathers.

The retrospect on this Jubilee occasion carries us back to the days of the great spiritual awakening. As we look back to those days, we are conscious of a painful contrast between what was then in the religious life of this people and what is now. We are conscious that the spiritual forces at work to-day among Hawaiians are not at all commensurate with those of fifty years ago. We are conscious that these spiritual forces are less advantageously located than formerly; that the masses of the people are less accessible to Gospel truth; that there is a notable absence of that eagerness to listen to the Gospel message which characterized the pungent preaching of the early days; that the current preaching of the word is in a marked degree less efficacious and stimulating.

With all the spiritual momentum of such a profound awakening as agitated our Hawaiian communities, under the labors of the missionary fathers, a half century of Christian endeavor under all ordinary conditions ought to show results quite different from those we see about us. The great Christian public in other lands, conversant with the historical facts of the evangelization of the Hawaiian race, would naturally expect a development of religious life in keeping with the phenomenal emergence from heathenism into Christian belief and practice- Under all ordinary conditions, the Hawaiian Churches to-day ought to show evidence of spiritual growth and stability adequately proportional to the expenditure in money and service in establishing these Churches.

That this is not the result is due to the fact that Christian life among the native population has been subjected to extraordinary conditions.

Industrial necessities have completely transformed the social status of Hawaiians. Owing to enhanced property values, and the organization of new centers of industry, Hawaiians have parted with their lands, have abandoned in some considerable degree the localities once occupied by them, have put themselves into industrial relations with people of dissimilar temperament and manner of life, have disjointed their relation to the Churches and Sunday schools owing to removal or to the contagious indifferentism of plantation life, and have so withdrawn from the simple contentedness of their former method of life as to take on new necessities and to adopt new ways that are a direct hindrance to Gospel effort among them.

Then, again, there has been a steady drain away from the sources at work to perpetuate and establish Christianity among this people.

The missionary fathers have dropped one by

one, and no one has come in to take their place. Effort has not been lacking on the part of Christian men and women, but it has been somewhat intermittent, and much less personal and definite than the work of the fathers. Somehow it has been overlooked in this sad experiment, that religion is a vitally personal matter. It cannot be transferred from parent to child as a physical trait or feature. Each generation must feel the impact of Gospel truth in the consciousness of its own necessities and surroundings. Because one generation or two have been moved by the appeals of consecrated men, and have made notable progress in Christian understanding and practice, it does not follow that such momentum will carry the next generation along the same channel. Especially is it necessary that such generation should be under the sway of forces adapted to its needs, when the population thus influenced has a constant gravitation toward heathenism.

The present is an era of spiritual declension and moral obliquity, very largely because there has been no adequate reinforcement of the work of other days. Unfortunately the momentum of the early work has not carried this people safely through the trying ordeal of maintaining religious belief and practice in the face of the large influx of ungodly men from Christian lands who have not only poisoned the simple faith of other days but have led the way back to vicious and abandoned lives.

The appeal to sense is stronger than the appeal to spirit. Passion outbids principle in the struggle for supremacy. What else ought we to expect in the circumstances than just what is daily transpiring before our eyes? Moral and spiritual forces are losing their grip on the native race, not because the Hawaiian people are not susceptible to Gospel truth, but because the forces employed to offset and counteract the tremendous downward tendency are shamefully inadequate. But of far greater importance than this steady diminution of forces, and the social and industrial revolution in Hawaiian life, is the absence of the profoundly consecrated spirit of the fathers. It was this spirit which initiated the work among Hawaiians; which brought the nation back to the Christian faith after repeated declensions; that sustained and nurtured the spiritual life of this people during the brightest period in its history. The tone of discouragement and of doubt as to the spiritual recuperation of our Hawaiian Churches is not born of a confident trust in God's purpose toward this people. It is not in keeping with the remarkable response to recent efforts in the interests of Hawaiian Christianity. The element that is needed to vitalize all effort in behalf of Hawaiians is a consecrated spirit that sees in the predominant Godlessness a Gospel opportunity; that fully recognizes the power of Gospel truth and that it is competent to change the whole complexion of things as they are, and to usher in an era of righteousness and of spiritual growth; that allows full play to the underlying principle in this whole matter that the descendants of the missionaries and their coadjutors in religious work are largely responsible for the perpetuation of Christian endeavor among the aborigines of these Islands.

This obligation cannot be shifted though it may and should be shared by the descendants of those who sustained the early missionaries in this field. God has not culminated His work in behalf of this people. The Gospel is yet the power of God unto salvation, to the Hawaiian first, and also to all the races that seek these shores. Well might Paul have been dismayed at the eloquent and refined and all-pervasive heathenism of the vast Roman Empire. But in the light of his courageous faith and confident belief in God's purpose and power, we may well bow ourselves in humiliation if we halt or hesitate in redeeming our obligation to this people in their hour of sorest need.

In a very true sense, the mass of Hawaiian Christians are oblivious to the pressing spiritual necessity that is upon them. The drift of the present spiritual declension is not understood by the average Hawaiian, and how can he be awake to a spiritual need of which he is unconscious? The responsibility to provide for this unconscious spiritual need rests on the resident descendants of the missionaries and their natural allies in Christian work.

There is a generation of Hawaiians almost, if not quite, ready for citizenship, who have been practically without the means of Gospel instruction and incentive. The windward side of Hawaii has now one native pastor, where a few years ago there were two foreign and four native pastors of

Hawaiian Churches. Is it any wonder that Churches are closed and every little hamlet is a rendezvous for heathen orgies when helpful religious forces are withdrawn from such regions? The days have surely come, of which Amos prophesied, when he said: "Behold the days come, saith the Lord God, that I will send a famine in the land, not a famine of bread, nor a thirst for water, but of hearing the words of the Lord."

The outlook should not dismay us. Is it not written—"When the enemy shall come in like a flood, the Spirit of the Lord shall lift up a standard against him?"

It will avail little if we fix our minds on the dark phases of religious effort here. What we need is to imbibe the spirit of the fathers, and gather up our strength and courage for aggressive work of a more pronounced type than we have known here in recent years.

We must not mistake the measure of our responsibility for the maintenance of Christian effort among Hawaiians. The decay of Christian faith and practice among our native population means the overthrow of Christian institutions in this land. Let this people recede into heathenism, or what is nearly as bad, a condition of chronic indifferentism, and we shall have very speedily a state of society that will not nurture even among our foreign residents anything more than an emasculated faith that is oppressed with the pervading unbelief like the scant righteousness of a miserable Lot fleeing to the hills for safety from the common destruction. The evangelization of the native race is to-day the key to the problem of how best to reach with Gospel incentives the races among us that are waiting in dumb heathenism for the blessed tidings of salvation and eternal life. How can we hope for any large success in the evangelization of our Oriental population when we offer them the Gospel in full view of a decadent Christianity among Hawaiians? We must work for the native race if we would save the other races among us.

It is only too common a remark among us: "Well, what is the use? This is a dying race. Its days are numbered, and to what purpose is all this waste of money and service?"

Observe how spiritually paralyzing this conviction is in all lines of Christian effort. It takes the edge off of all aggressive endeavor in behalf of the race, and renders abortive much that is undertaken in its interest. It is moreover a most ill-advised and unchristian prejudice. For our religion is not for races but for individuals irrespective of race, and so far as Christian obligation is concerned were there but one solitary Hawaiian left among us, the responsibility would be none the less strenuous to provide for his conversion and progress in Christian life. We cannot treat, in any light way, the obligation to promote Christian influences among the 40,000 aborigines of this land. It may, or may not be true, that this people are destined to extinction. That has nothing to do, either way, with the responsibility to forward their moral and spiritual welfare. We have present with us a generation of needy souls who have always been very largely dependent on the foreign population for religious stimulus and support. That dependence is more marked today than ever before. It is the measure of our responsibility. We shall prove recreant to our spiritual inheritance if we do not accept this responsibility on this suggestive occasion with renewed consecration. It is the legacy of the fathers to us, the children of another generation.

We may rightfully look to the home-land for substantial support. Our brethren across the water are responsible with us for the perpetuity of vital religious forces here. It is indeed difficult to see how they can be exempted from a very important share in this responsibility. But to us who are here, the responsibility assumes a personal character of no mean proportions. It means a close identification with the Hawaiian Churches and Sunday Schools. It means great patience and a courageous steadfastness in the face of most disheartening obstacles. It means a wrestling in prayer for a nation in peculiar jeopardy. It means a spirit of self-sacrifice in order that the ever-widening breach between foreigners and natives may be minimized. It means less of luxury in our homes and simpler habits for us all to allay the growing passion for display among the younger generation of Hawaiians.

And to-night as we turn our eyes from the remarkable fortitude and patience, the tactful wisdom and consecrated service of the fathers who so gladly gave their lives to the evangelization of their people, and turn our faces toward the future with all its spiritual possibilities, let us humbly acknowledge Him whose spirit possessed the fathers, and must evermore possess our souls if we are to cope successfully with the heavy personal responsibility that falls to-day on every Christian believer in this Island realm.

---o---

GLIMPSES OF HOME LIFE DURING THE FIRST DECADE OF THE MISSION.

BY MRS. LYDIA BINGHAM COAN.

First as to number in the list of honored names of missionaries to the Sandwich Islands, stands that of our beloved father, Rev. Hiram Bingham. Truly first pioneer, as no other name precedes his in American Board annals, as volunteer to enter this benighted land.

A voyage of 175 days in a small crowded brig, brought my parents and their associates to these shores on the 14th of April, 1820. They were not allowed to land until the 19th. Without furniture, bating one or two chairs and their trunks and chests, without crockery, except a supply of broken refuse articles sent with them from Boston, without domestics to aid them in their work, or markets at which to find provisions, these brave New England folk began their house-keeping in rude native huts, not far from the site of the old Bethel. No acqueducts brought water to their door; no wood was at hand for cooking. This was brought from the mountains upon the shoulders of the natives, and purchased at an extravagant price. The accumulated washing of the six months' voyage was carried to the field by the missionary wives to be done by themselves, and on the second day's exposure to the tropical sun the skin was blistered quite off my mother's arms.

In the midst of the pressing labor to adapt themselves to their new surroundings, came a demand to them from the chiefs, for superfine broadcloth garments to be made up, and six ruffled shirts with plaited bosoms. A task they cheerfully rendered for the sake of gaining the confidence and favor of the people.

With loving tact and patience my mother soon secured the attendance of thirty pupils at the school to be held in the one room of their humble dwelling—thus, as it were, planting the seed that blossoms now in Kawaiahao Seminary. Glance with me for a moment at the picture of this room as I find it sketched by my mother's pen on the 30th of June. "A room twenty feet square, where all eat, where two beds are, where thirteen persons stay, where yesterday were piled thirty mats, one hundred tapas, one hundred cocoanuts, a quantity of calabashes, six chair frames; while numbers were crowding around to look on."

Among their increasing comforts was this chair,* fashioned by my father's hands out of odd pieces of wood as he was able to pick them up, or as some one kindly gave a piece. In course of time the missionaries were, with some reluctance, allowed a bit of Honolulu's then arid plain whereon

---

*,The chair stood upon the platform, near the reader, at the Jubilee celebration.

to build the first frame house erected at the Islands. The materials for this were brought from Boston on the brig Thaddeus. The house is the low, white structure just opposite Kawaiahao Seminary.

Turning again to my mother's journal, we find a varied scene as she opens the door for our inspection. The year was 1823. Mr. Ellis, the English missionary, with two gentlemen, constituting a missionary deputation, had come with seven Tahitians to visit the new mission at Honolulu, and were the guests of the mission family. "*Four* distinct families, united in one. all having children, all having infants, with eighteen or twenty native children divided among them, two native youths, and one young man, Mr. H., from New England, formed at that time the mission family. One framed house containing *five* rooms, with some open space, above and below, with a store-room and eating room on the cellar ground, was the habitation in which the four families dwelt, and in which they sought to make comfortable their welcome guests. One of the five rooms was considered as necessary for common resort, for conversation, for the discussion of the language, to receive company, often calling, to attend morning and evening prayers, etc. Four were left, in which to place the beds of the eight parents and their little ones, and accommodate the gentlemen, (two of them desiring separate beds). Mr. and Mrs. C. have six children. They left their room, and with mats, contrived a little place above from the space left unfinished—there they spread their bed and dispose their children. Joining their apartment, one of the same size and structure is fitted to accommodate Mr. H. with his lodgings and various tools for repairing watches, etc., for the good of the public. On the opposite end of the house was the pretty room done off last fall for Mr. B. and myself. This in the bustle of the family we considered *our home*. We were happy to appropriate it to the accommodation of Mr. Bennet, while Messrs. Tyreman and Ellis had their beds in Mr. C.'s room below. I made the room very clean, put up the toilette, white curtains at the windows, etc., made a disposition of Mr. Bennet's many trunks and books, removing all our own, and shut the door, happy that it was in our power to make so comfortable such a visitor. All seemed settled now but Mr. Bingham and Sybil. Where is a spot for them? They have learned to do with little and will not require much. There was a space in the upper half story, the two ends appropriated as you have seen. The roof was low, but a field-bed could stand, and still a comfortable passage-way be between it and the head of the stairs. There was a small window between the roof and the floor, of six panes of glass, where I could set one or two trunks and turn around. Attached to this was a small spot which was under the roof, containing all the medical stores of the mission. This was our home through the summer. There was noise about us, and it needed some prudence, with a little one and three native children to maintain the character of good neighbors. A family of six children from which nothing separated but curtains and mats, a gentleman's room, into which company, native and foreign, was calling often, and two servants up and down the stairs, faithfully attending; a goldsmith's shop drawing company of some kind more or less every day; the family below keeping most of their chests of bedding and clothing somewhere in this loft; it may well be supposed there could be but little time when it could be said to be still around us. Yet here we all could have been comparatively comfortable had it not been for the burning sun of June and July, beating upon the roof and unclapboarded sides of the house. Ways and means must be devised, and labor done, that so many might be fed each day with food convenient for them. * * * I stood at the helm for a time and saw that fifty were fed with something regularly, three times a day. * * * We sometimes had beef, pork, potatoes, butter, cheese, flour, sugar, and sometimes were destitute of all of them, and of the most of them at a time. But whatever might have been the fare, a bystander would have pronounced it a cheerful meal. Though we sometimes wrought hard, and fared coarsely, yet God was pleased to allow no calamity to befall us, but gave us daily the hope that we were strengthening one another's hands in holding up the standard, which in His kind providence had been unfurled in this distant land."

There were many changes in this home as the years passed on. Three of the families constituting the household during the scenes just described, were, before long, established at other stations. But for our parents it was a permanent abode until they left in 1840. As one reinforcement after another arrived, this home was always open to receive and refresh them. And always was it the custom at such times to gather in the plain little parlor and give thanks to God that fresh, strong helpers had come to take hold of the work. Mother's duties were miscellaneous beyond description. In those early days were begun the hospitalities which have so long been a marked feature at Honolulu. The king and high chiefs were not infrequently her guests. Commanders and officers of men-of-war were often at her table, and her ever constant attentions were cheerfully extended to all, from the sovereign to the subject, from commander to sailor.

Aided by her missionary sisters she sometimes had under her superintendence between two and three hundred school children. It was under her personal direction and oversight that the *adobe* school building near the Stone Church was built. But the Church was of later date. We used to worship in a large, thatched meeting house, and I remember that mother's chair, and little chairs for ourselves were carried over Sabbath mornings and placed upon a platform in front of the pulpit. It must have been in this grass house that she used to meet the fifteen hundred women whose names she had upon roll-call, for "prayer, advice and exhortation." Mrs. Dr. Judd has told me how she and mother often threaded the narrow footpaths about the Nuuanu taro-patches as they went forth to visit among the crowded native huts. The beautiful homes in the valley now cover the ground so faithfully traversed by their weary feet. My father was the object of much wrath among wicked white men visiting the port of Honolulu. In 1826 occurred a scene never effaced from the memory of those who witnessed it. On a Sabbath, as my father was about to conduct the afternoon services, held in the house of Kalanimoku, squads of angry seamen, some of them intoxicated, began breaking in the windows. Others directed their steps towards our home where the mother was alone with her little girl. As father hastened to her protection, he fell into the hands of the riotous men, one of whom exclaimed, "Here he is; I have got him; come on." An Irishman, brandishing his knife in his face, with angry earnestness said: "*You* are the *man every* day." Suddenly one of them aimed a spiteful blow with a club at his head. This was a signal for resistance which the devoted pupils, John Ii and others, were quick to improve. The rioters were seized, disarmed and bound. But another company were soon on hand to vent their rage. One broke in a window, and another left marks of his club upon the door panels, and while two were applying their strength to force it open, one turned savagely upon his comrade and dealt him a blow that felled him to the ground.

Twice in these early years the dear parents were called to the tender sorrow of laying away their babes from their sight. Over the little grave of the elder one were held the first rites of

Christian burial ever observed in this land. Twice it was theirs to experience a sorrow almost as keen as that of the grave. The eldest born and her sister were sent forth from their loving arms to the care of friends 18,000 miles away. Allow me again to read to you from our mother's own words, written under the pangs of parting: "I make hard work of this business. Are we called to put this little, giddy, affectionate thing from us? You cannot tell what a question it is, every hour of the day, on my mind. We are, indeed, taking our steps forward as though the path was clear, but it is constantly with a kind of scant hope of retracing them. * * * January 5th. A heavy day. We have packed two little chests—sent them aboard. The clock has struck nine. The bustling house is stilled. My little ones are sleeping quietly by. Think you how I look upon one of them. The prattling voice, after one more morning comes, will probably fall on my ears no more. Her thoughtless, youthful steps,—who will guide them? Her portion of life's bitter cup— who will sweeten? But why these inquiries of my fluttered spirit? My heart does rest in God. My hope is there. On His covenanted mercy I cast this little wanderer from a mother's bosom. Having this blessed privilege my song shall be of praise."

Later in life, referring to these trials, she wrote, "Through the days of their childhood while under the paternal roof, such was the demand for direct effort to be made among the women and children of the land, in bringing them into schools, moral associations, etc., that we felt we were called upon by the providence of God to give the strength and the time to direct labors among them, which our maternal feelings coveted for our own precious offspring. It is impossible to describe the struggle sometimes in our breast between the mother's feelings, and what appeared to be a special and almost unparalleled call from the people for all the energy of which the poor frame and burdened mind were capable.

Away from the heat and noise of the dusty plain, our parents sometimes resorted for brief rest to the cool spring and quiet nook of Punahou, a gift to them in fee simple from the high-chief Boki. That he might aid in establishing a school for missionary children, and thus save others from experiences so trying as those of sending their little ones to the United States, father donated this pleasant tract of land, a spot that might have been his childrens' inheritance, to the American Board, as a site for Oahu College.

Our father's life passed in labors most abundant. To him it was granted to exert a strong influence over the high chiefs, guiding them by wise counsels as they took their first steps towards enlightened, Christian government. His it was, with his coadjutors, to reduce the barbarous language to writing, and to give the Hawaiians the Bible in their own tongue. Their first hymns were from his pen—both translations and original ones—for which, sweet singer that he was, he composed some of the tunes. Again and again, he was absent on tours among the natives; or summoned, now and then, to distant stations as the only one to whom those in need could look for medical help. When the press was established in the old printing house, it was his keen, dark eye that watched its work most continuously, and scanned thousands of pages of proof-sheets. In the midst of such heroic tasks, his fingers with cunning skill sometimes relieved the tired brain by fashioning furniture and toys for household use and children's play—a chair for the Queen, settees and book case for mother, windmills and dolls for us. For one windmill he wrote this little verse:

"Gentle breezes bid me go;
Swift their summons I'll obey.
So should children quickly do
What their parents wish or say."

Long cherished among our treasures we have kept the wooden dolls that were all we had in our childhood days at the Islands. Is not this care proof that we loved them very dearly? Let me show you the quaint little group as we have brought them on this anniversary day out of stowed-away chests, where they have quietly lain for years, in faded, old-fashioned garb.

In closing, may I again revert to this old armchair? In it Kings and Queens have sat. Probably every missionary lady at the Islands, prior to 1840, has found it a seat of ease and restfulness. To the seven children, that one after another, nestled in our gentle mother's arms, were sung their lullabyes, as here she rocked them to sleep. Slung on poles and borne on the shoulders of willing bearers, it was her carriage as, once and again, she

made the tour of Oahu. Taken with us around
Cape Horn to the States, it waited six years for
lodgement in a home where the scattered family
could once more be gathered together as a household. Nine months of sweet content with our
feeble, blessed mother were given us before her
weary pilgrimage ended; and then, sitting in this
chair, even as she had wished she might be when
the end should come, and with praises on her lips
for Him who cared for her, she calmly breathed her
life out and went home to God and Heaven.

―――o―――
HILO IN 1832.

BY MRS. D. B. LYMAN.

[Written by Mrs. Lyman in 1883.]

As I have been requested to give some reminiscences of our missionary life, I would begin by
saying that, after a sojourn of six weeks in Honolulu we came to Hilo in July, 1832, and for fifty-
one years this has been our home. The Hilo of
the present day is very different from what it
was on our arrival here. Then there were
no foreign residents save the missionaries
who had preceded us. There was but one
frame building in all this region, and that was the
one which was built by Mr. Goodrich, and which
the Coans have occupied. There were no roads
(only foot paths), no fences, and the Wailuku
river was crossed on a plank; and the only bell in
the place hung in a breadfruit tree; and I might
add there were no trees except the breadfruit,

which were abundant and in a flourishing condition, and a fringe of cocoanut trees along the shore. The people were numerous and had a healthy look; they were docile, and very friendly. Nearly all were clad in their native costume as they had no means of obtaining foreign cloth. A few schooners owned by the chiefs, came here occasionally, not to bring blessings to the natives, but to levy contributions of kapa, mats, dried fish, pigs, etc.

On our arrival here the natives flocked around us, giving us a sincere and hearty welcome. We were initiated into our work by Mr. and Mrs. Green, who had been laboring here about two years, but who soon after left to commence a new station at Wailuku, on Maui. On their leaving, Mr. and Mrs. Dibble, who had been co-laborers with the Greens, returned from Honolulu where they had been detained by sickness, and so long as they remained we were intimately associated in our labors for the people. The gentlemen were associate pastors, and as soon as Mr. Lyman had sufficient command of the language to preach, they took turns in spending the Sabbaths at the two out-stations of Kuolo and Hakalau. Small churches had been erected there and a goodly number assembled in them on the Sabbath.

Together they traversed the districts of Puna and Hilo on foot, preaching the Gospel, examining schools, and doing what lay in their power to keep up the interest which had been awakened among the natives. When at home they had no idle moments. From early dawn till the stars came out, there were demands on their time, and yet things were so systematized that the machinery worked without friction. What with attending meetings, teaching school, visiting among the people and receiving visits from them at stated seasons, they had very little leisure.

Meantime, the ladies were similarly employed as their husbands, with the exception of touring and preaching. We had our meetings and schools for the women and children, and entertained those who were disposed to call and see us in our homes, and their number was legion, and their calls were so protracted as sometimes to try our patience a little. All those who came in from Puna and Hilo invariably visited the mission families; some would come in large companies, others in families (and there were some large families of sons and daughters in those days). But this gave us an opportunity of making the acquaintance of those living remote from us, so that in process of time we knew the names of very many people in both districts, and among them were the old priest and priestess of Pele, who never failed to visit us when here. Those were the halcyon days when we were permitted to do the work for which we came without let or hindrance, and they are now remembered with unfeigned pleasure.

A word about the buildings used in connection with our missionary work.

When we came, the Haili Church, a remarkably large and well-built structure, was standing near our present Court House, or between that and Dr. Kittredge's, and would accommodate four or five thousand people compactly seated on the ground. Our own house, built after our arrival and for aloha, stood just above the Foreign Church. [A beautiful tamarind tree of my own planting, had afterwards to be cut down to make room for the Foreign Church, and possibly the stump is still under that building). The house was a common thatched building with no floor, and only coarse mat partitions, but we were more fortunate than some of our missionary friends in having some glass windows made by Mr. Lyman, as were the window and door frames. No palace was ever more highly prized than was this humble dwelling, for we felt that after months of wandering we were "home at last," and could now give ourselves wholly to the work of the Lord. Our associates occupied another humble dwelling just mauka of ours, which stood close to the road that now leads to Mr. Baker's. [It was a house that had a history, and I may allude to it again.]

The house in which most of our schools were kept, stood half-way between ours and Mrs. Dibble's, near where the road running to the shore now is [or Church street.] There was another one where the "lunas" [elders, deacons] and better sort of men were taught.

There were schools at Puneo, Piihonua, Kukuau, and Waiakea, taught by natives [Everybody went to school in those days.] but the pupils at the station schools were more select than those of others. We were not slow to perceive that our predecessors had planned intelligently, and labored faithfully and successfully. The school system was admirable for the times, there being school buildings through the two districts at convenient distances for all to attend [and they did pretty generally attend], and *all*, whose eyes were not dim with age, learned to read. Each school had two sets of teachers, and whilst one set was teaching, the other was here attending the teachers' school which was taught by the missionaries. When we came there were nearly eighty teachers in the school. Parts of the Bible had been translated and were used in the schools. We believed that the way to convert a nation was to give them the Bible in their own language, and that the easiest way of getting it into circulation was to introduce it into the schools. The result was that in a few years the people became intelligent readers of the Bible, and some of those living in the immediate vicinity of the mission station good Biblical scholars. Scripture maps on a large scale interested them much and helped them to a better understanding of what they read. The teachers were instructed and aided in making large maps for their school rooms to accompany the new geography, which they took home with them for the first time, and this greatly elevated the teachers in the eyes of their pupils, and gave a new impulse to the schools. And here let me say that if my recollection serves me, only one of those faithful teachers had any foreign garments. neither had they any compensation for teaching. It was an honor to be appointed a teacher, besides, their desire to increase learning, was a sufficient inducement to engage in teaching. And they were truly ambitious of having their schools make a good show when they were visited and examined by the missionaries, as they were for many years. Thus we lived and labored till the fall of 1834, when Mr. Dibble was obliged to take his family to Lahaina for medical aid, and the climate agreeing with him better there, he being of consumptive habit, decided to remain and teach in the Seminary in Lahainaluna. This was a sore trial to us. Mr. Goodrich and wife were still here, but the health of neither permitted them to do much direct missionary work. Besides, they were making preparations to return with their growing family to the States. In the spring of 1835, a new reinforcement arrived at Honolulu, during the annual meeting of the mission. As we were to have new associates, we made known our preference for Mr. and Mrs. Coan, and the request was granted. And, as is well known, we stood shoulder to shoulder for many years in the work at Hilo.

For some two or three years the subject of a boys' boarding school had been discussed at the annual meetings, and all were desirous to have the experiment tried. No one however was ready to engage in such doubtful work.

At the meeting in 1836, it was decided that the experiment be tried at Hilo, leaving it for the brethren to decide as to who should develop the much desired thing. The great object in view was to train more intelligent teachers for the common schools. So, on returning home, a conference was held, and it was decided that as Mr. Coan was not particularly fond of teaching, and

Mr. Lyman had had considerable experience in that line, he take the school. But there was not the semblance of a house for it. I find it recorded that on the 18th day of August, 1836, the site for a house was selected. It was to be 64 x 24 feet; to contain a study for Mr. L., a school room, dining room, pantry, and nine lodging rooms, and to be finished in three or four weeks. The posts were set in the ground, the whole building was thatched and the partitions were of coarse matting. It was on the day the building was commenced that we took our first scholar, but waited for others till it was completed.

We were then living in the house, now occupied by Dr. Wetmore, which we had built the previous year, so our school house stood just mauka of Dr. Wetmore's present dwelling. Before the close of September we opened our school with a small number of scholars. The parents were fearful, as it was to be a manual labor school, and before the close of the year, four boys were taken away. All came to us in a very destitute condition, and we were obliged to furnish sleeping kapa, mats, shirts and pants, which we required them to wear from the first, and were all ready when they came. The boys, though at first quite wild, were soon toned down, submitted to the rules of the school readily, and made commendable progress in their studies, and so the problem was being solved.

So well pleased were the parents with the appearance of the school, that the second year they were quite anxious for us to take their boys, and when we had enlarged our accommodations, and the best boys were selected from the six different districts of the Island, they would come in such crowds at the time appointed for receiving new scholars, that we found it very difficult to decide which of them should enter, and who be sent home for lack of room. Many a poor fellow has turned away with tears in his eyes and with a firm resolve to get in the ensuing year, and he pretty generally succeeded.

For several years our mail matter was sent by whale ships which were fitted out in the fall of the year—consequently our letters and publications were from a year to eighteen months old, on being received.

The house that was, and is not, but which has a history. Said house was built by Rev. J. S. Green about the year 1830. The walls were of stone and plastered; the roof was thatched. At first it had but two rooms, but afterwards another was added. Mr. Green's family occupied the house till they left Hilo in 1832, then the Dibbles lived in it about two years, or till they left the station in 1844; we then exchanged our thatched cottage for this more pretentious building, where we remained more than a year, and till the house now occupied by Dr. Wetmore was ready for use. During that time came Mr. and Mrs. Coan, and they kept house for three months in the rear end of this stone building, then they moved in.o the house just vacated by Mr. Goodrich.

The January following we removed to our new dwelling, and the next year we commenced the "Hilo Boarding School." The little stone house was then used for schools and meetings, till the arrival of Mr. and Mrs. Wilcox, in the summer of 1838; it was then fitted up for their use.

As the number of pupils increased, we found the place too strait for us; so we were advised to erect new buildings for ourselves and for the school, on a new site, which we did, taking possession of them in April, 1839.

The Wilcoxes moved into the house which we vacated, and the little stone house was fitted up for schools, meetings, etc. One partition being removed it made a good sized school room, and so long as the Wilcoxes remained here, it was used for that purpose.

In those early days but few whaleships visited our harbor, never more than one or two in a season. Sabbath services were held for them at one or the other of the mission houses, and not unfrequently nearly the whole ship's company would be present. As the shipping increased, larger accommodations were needed, so the stone building was fitted up with seats and a desk, and covered with cloth over head, and was then dignified by the name of "Seamen's Chapel," and there Sabbath services were held during the shipping season, and sometimes between seasons.

The first foreign Sabbath School was organized in April, 1853, Mr. Stevens, a gentleman from Boston, being the superintendent.

Larger accommodations being needed for the Wednesday evening prayer meeting, which had always been held in private houses, it was finally located in this lowly dwelling, the house being lighted by lamps carried by the attendants. But the crowning act of all was the formation of the Foreign Church in January, 1868, with a few members, and the Communion was administered, a memorable day.

The next day the house was demolished and the stones were used for the underpinning of the present Foreign Church building.

———o———

THE WORK OF REV. J. S. GREEN ON MAUI.

Rev. J. S. and Mrs. T. A. Green were natives of the State of Connecticut.

The former graduated at Andover Theological Seminary in 1827. They left Boston as missionaries, under the auspices of the American Board, Nov. 3, 1827, and reached the Sandwich Islands March 31, 1828. The long voyage was replete with experiences of most trying nature; but never once did they lose faith in God—never once regret the all important step they had taken—a step for life.

In 1829, Mr. Green visited the North West Coast, for the purpose of ascertaining whether missionary stations might be established among the Indians there.

During his absence of nine months, Mrs. Green, while enduring the many hardships incident to early missionary life, was called to part with their only child, Beriah.

In 1830, they removed to Lahaina. In 1831, to Hilo. In 1832, to Wailuku. In 1835, while they were at Honolulu, their third child, Emily, died from the effects of a distressing accident. During the years spent at these four missionary posts of labor, their efforts were unceasing both day and night in imparting instruction to the people. Translating, preaching, teaching, house visiting— every nerve was strained to the utmost in efforts to improve the condition of the people. The boarding school for Hawaiian girls at Wailuku, Maui, was a great blessing, and its influence is still felt.

In 1842, after many sleepless nights, and days of prayerful consideration and deliberation, they left the service of the A. B. C. F. M., and cast themselves upon the people of Makawao district for a support. They were convinced that the relations the Board sustained to American slavery was not right in the sight of God. So, leaving their Wailuku home and its comforts, they became pioneers once more, never losing their cheerful trust in the good Providence that had provided for their daily wants. The history of all they endured—all they did for the sake of their children, and the people of their charge, is a thrilling one.

On the 6th of October, 1859, the beloved wife and mother passed away, gently as a babe to rest. She seemed as an *angel* amongst us; the music of her voice so sweet, the light in her eye so heavenly; all the suffering, self-denial, cheery hopefulness, most marked—even in the midst of most intense physical sufferings, always making *the best* of whatever came to her—until we could clearly see the Refiner's image reflected in her face. It was to her an inestimable privilege to spend and be spent for her beloved Savior.

In 1860, Mr. Green and daughter went to the States. To the soul of the devoted lover of his country it was "a feast of fat things;" the reunion with his aged father, and the many with whom he had corresponded during the long period of separation. On every hand he met with those who knew him through his communications with the press. His enthusiasm knew no bounds as he became personally familiar with the varied incidents of the *war* that ended *American slavery*. He was *posted* on the political, moral, and religious phases of American history, and *had* been during all his life of missionary abnegation. His son's arrival East, completed the happiness, long anticipated by him, when his children should be allowed the joy of treading his country's soil.

On the 11th of September, 1861, Mr. Green was united in Marriage to Miss A. C. Spring, of Brimfield, Massachusetts. Shortly after they set forth for the Islands, and in due time were at home, heartily in earnest for their chosen work. The pleasure of the people in welcoming them was most delightfully expressed by their "aloha"— and various gifts. The following is a later insertion: The present Mrs. Green has been to her family, and to the people of Mr. Green's parish, a good gift, sent specially from God to comfort and to bless. Her missionary life has been one of entire consecration to the master's service. The traits of character that rendered the first Mrs. Green peculiarly adapted to sustain well the relation of wife, mother, friend, are *hers*. Prov. 31 : 28.

At my special request, daughter Mary has prepared the foregoing memorial of her venerated parents, to which I will add a few items in reference to her beloved father's never failing zeal for the benefit of immortal souls, which included not only Hawaiians, but English speaking foreigners.

For many years previous to his Eastern trip in 1860–1, he conducted Sabbath morning services for the latter at his own residence; and on his return—for sixteen years, in a pleasant little Church erected while absent. Besides Makawao, his mission field—until he was enfeebled by age—extended from Euelo to Keokea and Kalepolepo, a distance of thirty miles. The out-stations were visited quarterly. His Sabbath labors were arduous. At sunrise he was invariably found at the Native Church, for a season of prayer with the few who resided in the immediate vicinity. Sabbath school was held at noon, when all participated in repeating the Scriptures learned during the preceding week; some, even children, were able to recite whole chapters; questions and answers followed; then a two hours preaching service. The first Monday in each month was observed as the monthly concert of prayer for the conversion of the world, and the last, for those of all lands "in bonds." Every Wednesday afternoon he had what he called a "school." The exercises were in theology, Hawaiian grammar, and Church history.

Great was Mr. Grean's joy when King Kamehameha III permitted his subjects to become proprietors of the soil, and as his supervisor he disposed of 1,400 acres. He expended much time and toil in teaching agriculture, and the possibility of acquiring comfortable homes, telling them there was no reason why every man should not "sit under his own vine and fig tree," but from neglect to plant them! Not less was his deep *sorrow*, when for a few pieces of silver, they aimlessly returned to their former habits of life.

The decadence of the people was another source of grief; and, in seasons of any prevalent disease, he interested himsel in ascertaining what might be preventives, as well as remedies. In 1870, when two hundred and thirty deaths were reported in his parish from fever, he wrote to a friend,—"We are reminded, daily, that what we do for the Hawaiian race must be done quickly, for they are fast going to the grave. It is a time of sickness—a dying time. Pray for the poor remnant of an interesting nation, that they may all become righteous."

After such abundant labors, is it surprising that within three months of an anticipated "jubilee," the silver cord was loosed, the golden bowl was broken at the fountain, and the wheel broken at the cistern?

"Him that overcometh will I make a pillar in the temple of my God, and he shall go no more out, and I will write upon him the name of my God."

In Christian sympathy and love,
A. C. GREEN.

Makawao, March 31, 1887.

After reading this paper at the Jubilee meeting a friend of my father said that he thought something should have been said in connection with the remarks upon his interest in keeping the natives in possession and profitable employment of their lands, and of the part he took in the cultivation of wheat. Mr. Green was called the father of wheat culture on the island of Maui, and thence in the Islands. About the year 1851, a strong impulse had been given to the raising of wheat by the high price of flour. Mr. Green led the way in Makawao to what promised to be the establishment of a large and prosperous agricultural industry. The following extract from a report of his to the Royal Agricultural Society gives a vivid picture of his labors and hopes :—

"Two boys, of 14 to 16 years of age, perhaps of African and Hawaiian descent, have been my only helpers. They were handy in the management of oxen, and, besides doing most of my plowing, they took care of our cows and did the milking. The wheat land they plowed, and after lying awhile in the furrow, to allow the Kolea (a Hawaiian bird useful for the purpose) to destroy the crop of Pelua (caterpillars), we furrowed the field and gave it the second plowing. The Kolea gave the furrows another cropping, after which we prepared for sowing. * * * About the 10th of March I finished the sowing. So far, so good. For a few nights I rested well, free from care. But I soon found that my charge required a constant, well-nigh sleepless vigilance. The peelua, or cut worm, did me some damage, though not greater than I had reason to expect. But as we have no fences about our fields, watchfulness by day and by night against the intrusion of cattle and horses is indispensable. Scarcely a single night since the grain became high enough to attract the attention of cattle, has passed, in which I have not taken the rounds by moonlight and star-light or lamp-light, in the rains or during a cessation of a few moments to ascertain the state of things in relation to cattle. The last thing before lying down, and the first thing at dawn of day, is a walk to the most exposed places of my wheat field. Need I say that this is sober *prose*, not a particle of poetry in all this business of plowing, sowing and watching. The author of the "Song of the Shirt" would be the man to give us the song of the wheat in its earliest stages. Yet, Mr. Chairman, there is another side to the story—a bright side. There is the *poetry* of wheat raising. I felt something of it from the moment I cast in the first handful of this *prince* of grains. The thought, like the tones of a well-tuned instrument, thrilled through my bosom that I was engaged in a noble business, a business in which Paul or John might engage—were they on earth, without a single twinge of conscience or the shadow of a blush; a business, in a word, in which I could pray down a blessing from the Father of Mercies. * * * None is yet ripe—none will be at the time of the Fair; but as I rode around yesterday and examined nearly every field and patch that is growing at Makawao, my pleasure was exceeding great. To see a hundred acres of wheat at a glance waving to the winds, and this at the Sandwich Islands, caused me to bless the Great Proprietor of all and awaken the hope that I should see greater things than these."

There was a measure of success. Three wheat mills were built in different parts of the Islands. Native Hawaiians were successful wheat growers. But from inherent difficulties, which it would be interesting to discuss, if this were not a memoir, but an agricultural essay, the whole business within five or six years, failed and ceased entirely.

LAWRENCE McCULLY.

----o----

A MISSIONARY'S JOURNAL.

BY MRS. U. S. EMERSON.

On November 26, 1831, Mr. Emerson and I embarked from New Bedford on board the ship Averick, Captain Swain, for the Sandwich Islands. The company of which we formed a part, constituted the "fourth reinforcement" to these Islands. Our number was nineteen, as follows: Rev. Wm. P. Alexander and wife, Rev. Richard Armstrong and wife, Alonzo Chapin, M. D., and wife, Rev. John S. Emerson and wife, Rev. Cochran Forbes and wife, Rev. Harvey R. Hitchcock and wife, Rev. David B. Lyman and wife, Rev. Lorenzo Lyons and wife, Mr. Edmund Rogers, printer, Rev. Ephraim Spaulding and wife.

On the 17th of May, 1832, we anchored off Honolulu harbor, truly thankful that our long and painful voyage was ended. Messrs. Bingham and

Whitney came out to meet us on the ship and accompanied us ashore. The old mission wagon was in waiting at the beach, and Mrs. Armstrong and I entered it. We were drawn by a team of native men, pulling and pushing. This method of riding seemed so comical, that I could not suppress a laugh, but looking about and seeing the grave faces of Messrs. Bingham and Whitney, I perceived that they saw nothing unusual, and concluded it was time for me to put on my customary sober face. At Mr. Chamberlain's we met several of the missionaries, who had come to Honolulu from the other islands to attend the general meeting, which was to take place in June. Mr. Spaulding and Mr. Emerson and I were entertained at Mr. Clarke's. Mrs. Clarke had been my school mate in the States and the pleasure of being with her was not small. A clean, airy chamber with plenty of room to move in, the neatness of the table and food offered such a contrast to the accommodations on ship board, that we at once felt ourselves at home.

The next day our company went to the palace, a large grass house, and were introduced to the young King, Kauikeaouli, a pleasing youth, who was attended by the chiefs Keeaumoku, Princess Boki and Hoapili, Governor of Maui. Thence we went to the palace of the Queen Regent, Kaahumanu, who was ill and sitting in her arm chair. She received us cordially, and wept, giving as a reason, that it was because the Lord had so greatly blessed her people in sending them teachers of the good way of life. She was soon afterward carried to Manoa, where she lingered a little more than a week. and then passed away, June 5th, 1832, happy in the Christian's hope. Her death was a great loss to her people, as after her conversion in 1824, she was a firm friend of the missionaries, ready for every good work, a power in the land.

In July, we embarked on a small schooner for Waialua, the station assigned to Mr. Emerson and myself. We had no associate, but Mr. and Mrs. Clarke preceded us by a few days on horseback, to be with us until our knowledge of the Hawaiian language should enable us to get along alone. Providentially we were only one night on the ocean, a short passage. Laanui the local chief met us in his canoe and gave us a warm welcome. Mr. and Mrs. Clarke and their daughter Mary awaited us on the shore, and we were conducted to a small grass house prepared for our reception. I had to stoop on entering the door, and the only windows were holes, where the thatch had been removed, but it was our home, and I was happy. Laanui was a kind and thoughtful man, and did all in his power to supply our wants. He was also our teacher in the language, as he had been while we were in Honolulu. My husband would read his sermons to him before preaching. In about two months he preached his first Hawaiian sermon.

I soon commenced teaching the women in elementary arithmetic giving them such instruction as my poor acquaintance with the native tongue allowed. Each one brought a little bag of kakalaioa seeds to be used as counters in aiding their computations, of which they made hard work. Mrs. Clarke had a reading school. We also opened a singing school, which I continued for many years, having much better success with the younger ones than with the adults. Very soon after our arrival at Waialua the natives were ordered by the chief to build us a new, thatched house, in which we had three rooms partitioned by mats. The doors and windows were from an old house of Mr. Clarke's in Honolulu. They also built a separate house for Mr. Clarke, besides a small one for his study.

Mr. and Mrs. Clarke remained with us about five months and then returned to their Honolulu home. At first we felt very lonely, but were too busy to indulge in home sickness or regrets. Day schools and Sabbath schools for the children and adults and sewing schools for the women soon engaged my attention and kept me busy as a bee. Mr. Emerson was both pastor and superintendent of schools in three districts, of Waianae, Waialua and Koolauloa, this being the order in which they occur on the map, and he occasionally made tours from the central district in either direction. After Rev. Lowell Smith came to Ewa, he relieved him for a time of the charge of Waianae. At that time there were no suitable maps for use in teaching the Hawaiians, and as soon as practicable I projected a large map of the world for our classes. We also instructed some of the brightest scholars in the art of map making. Mr. Emerson having made maps of the different countries for his school of men. I have at the present time such a map of Kauai, copied by one of my older pupils. He was a bright promising youth, from whom we had hoped much, but falling sick, his family persisted in employing a native kahuna, and he died.

Our dining, which was also our sitting room, would of an evening often be crowded with natives, who had come for advice and to tell their thoughts (manao). Among them came Hewahewa, an old man, infirm and nearly blind, famous for having been the much dreaded high priest of Kamehmeha I. He had often accompanied the conqueror in his voyages of conquest from island to island, his office being to propitiate the war god, Kukailimoku, on the eve of battle with human sacrifices. The residence of this venerable savage was in the beautiful valley of Waimea. He expressed deep penitence for his past life, gratitude to the teachers, who had brought the new light, and mourned that the imperfection of his sight, the result of his own vices, would not permit him to acquire the art of reading. At the same time he declared himself resolved to devote the remainder of his days to the service of the true God. This was one of the many incidents, which encouraged us and cheered our hearts in our intercourse with this teachable, but fickle minded people-

In 1833, a larger and more substantial thatched house was built for public worship. The one previously used had stood upon the sea beach, and when the surf was high the noise of the waves interrupted the voice of the preacher. When the new

Church was completed Rev. Hiram Bingham and Dr. Judd came over to assist in its dedication.

At the same time a churh was organized, to which, as years went by, numbers were added from the out districts of Waianae and Koolauloa, the limits of Mr. Emerson's parish at this time extending over a coast of not less than fifty-eight miles. As time went on this was somewhat shortened up, and Waianae was put under the pastoral care of Rev. Lowell Smith, who with his lovely wife of blessed memory, were our nearest white neighbors. At their house in Ewa, so long as they remained there, we always enjoyed friendly reunions when we sought with them a resting place on our fatiguing horseback journeys to and from the annual General Meetings at Honolulu. In after years, when Rev. A. Bishop, occupied this station and was pastor of the Churches of Ewa and Waianae, we were often most pleasantly and hospitably entertained by him and his family.

A separate Church organization was afterwards formed at the beautiful village of Hauula (red dew), distant from the village of Waialua about twenty miles. Mr. Emerson, however, retained the pastoral charge of this new Church for many years, finally yielding it to Rev. M. Kaaea. In the year 1847 or 1848 the spiritual wants of the people were still further provided for by the organization of a Church at Kahuku, which in 1849 was put under the care of Rev. James Kekela, where he remained and did good and efficient work till his departure on the mission to the Marquesas Islands, in 1852. Kekela was a plain, unassuming man of excellent common sense and practical judgment. A good student and expositor of the Bible, and a wise pastor, qualities which made him an invaluable assistant to Mr. Emerson, and pointed him out as the very one to be selected to go as the first Hawaiian missionary to foreign shores. He had an excellent helper in his wife, Naomi.

It should be understood that, though separately organized, these Churches were still under my husband's general oversight, and looked up to him as their *makua*, father.

I have not the means at hand to give the number of Church members, received at different times, but by reference to my husband's journal, I am able to say that in the year 1838, 104 members were added to the Church at Waialua. Among the means that should be mentioned as greatly relied upon and immediately influential in securing these happy results, were "protracted meetings." My husband's journal alludes to one, which he held at Kahana, Koolauloa, with the assistance of native Christians. The work was a powerful one. The people said they had seen strange things. The mass of the population was greatly moved, and expressed the determination to come over to the Lord's side. This local manifestation of spiritual interest was a part of the great revival which extended over the whole group, and is usually known as the revival of 1838.

Some one will ask, what was the appearance of the congregation when assembled at Church in those olden times? Picture to yourselves a large thatched house, destitute alike of seats and board floor, instead of which we see the ground covered with rush mats, whereon sit rows of dark-skinned attentive listeners, of all ages and of both sexes. We have assembled before us almost the entire population of the district. Seated next to the missionaries is the chief, Laanui, who wears with dignity a suit of some black or blue cloth, the brass buttons of which have about them a military suggestion. The general dress of the people is, for the men, the malo and the kihei, knotted over one shoulder, with a ready acceptance of the shirt and pantaloons of civilization; and for the women, it is the pau and hihei, with a tendency towards the more complete covering of the person with the holoku. There is a plentiful sprinkling of grey heads, and many of the mothers have brought their babes in their arms with them. The attention and decorum of the audience is perfect, save that it is not the fashion for the Hawaiian to suppress a cough, and the attendance of numbers of dogs, who come as part of the family, creates a diversion, that would seriously try the gravity of a more civilized audience. But the dignity of the Hawaiian is something superb, and is not easily upset. It has been said that the proper costume of a Hawaiian savage was "a smile, a malo and a cutaneous eruption." The first Hawaiian man that came into our employ, had the malo, an old, borrowed shirt, and the cutaneous eruption, but as to the smile, he was sober as a judge. I can testify, that in the early days of my missionary life, I never saw a Hawaiian audience, whatever their costume, behave otherwise than with decorum and self possession. As a rule the Hawaiians, when seen in public, were neat in their persons and neat in their dress. As an illustration of their neatness at that time, it was the prevailing custom among a large number of the older adults for each person to bring a spittoon, as he came to Church, generally a simple gourd shell. This may have been the result of chiefish example and influence, and it may have arisen in part from fear of the power of the kahuna anaana, who sought something that had touched the body of the person in order to gain a supposed hold over him. The decorum and respectful attention of the Hawaiian audience at Church was due in part to the great awe and respect felt by them for the missionary, and in part was to be accounted for by the fact that they were in the presence of their chief, at whose command in many cases they went to the Church I must here remark, that the influence exercised by the chief, Laanui, and of the Konohiki, Kuakoa, was in general a good one, and such as to strengthen our hands.

But to return to the audience at Church. While the natives were in the habit of using frequent ablutions, for fresh water was abundant in the district, still there was much in their habits, which might cause offense to the fastidious senses of a civilized person. The use of the comb, for instance, to remove vermin from their abundant heads of hair had to be inculcated.

Of the work of later years, with its diligent

seed-sowing and fruitage, of the dawning in darkened minds of that light which shineth brighter and brighter unto the perfect day, of the founding of many Christian homes, of the forming of something like an enlightened Christian conscience in previously heathen communities, of the increasing physical prosperity of the people about us, of the lapse of some into revived forms of heathenism, of the struggle between superstition and faith for the mastery over the bodies and souls of the poor Hawaiians, of the progressive wasting and decimation of the native race by epidemics, which swept through their communities like fire through a prairie, or by endemic disease, which clung to them like a poisoned garment; of all these, which formed some of the lights and shadows in the picture of missionary life, I have not the time to speak.

The Hawaiians of to-day are no longer the teachable children of two generations ago, eager to seek advice and missionary counsel. This not to be expected. Of the seed sown the harvest has been plentiful. For this we thank God. While many dark clouds overshadow our dear Hawaii nei, we cannot but return thanks to Almighty God for having smiled upon the efforts thus far made to found a stable Christianity in the midst of this people, and trust his guidance and sustaining care to preserve it to the remotest generation.

THE WORK ON MOLOKAI.

BY MRS. R. H. HITCHCOCK.

Mr. Hitchcock, accompanied by Rev. Lorrin Andrews, of Lahainaluna, made the first call at Molokai while at Lahaina, improving his knowledge of the Hawaiian language under the instruction of Rev. Mr. Richard, missionary of the place. The site selected by the station was disapproved of by Geo. Adams, owner of the land. Mr. Hitchcock was requested by Hooapiliwahine to go again to Molokai and select a site for the station on her land, which he did, and it proved to be the best and most central for the island. Kekauluahi, King Lunalilo's mother, took Mr. Hitchcock, wife and infant son over the 7th of November, 1832, on her little sloop. A large thatched house had been built by the natives with three doors, no window or floor or partition. We were received with joy by the natives. Auhea, the chief who took us over, staid several days with us, meeting with the people, telling them what to do, obey the missionary, attend the meetings and take care of us. We were the only foreigners on Molokai then and for some time. There were many children, and people came a long way to meeting.

There was no meeting house or school house, no roads except the foot paths of the natives, no horses except a lame one belonging to a chief, no cattle until a cow was sent to us by the mission. Mr. Hitchcock's first pulpit was the broken stump of a lauhala tree on which was placed a board where he stood and preached while the people sat on the ground under the trees. There was scarcely a cloth garment of any kind to be seen in the congregation. Before many months had passed a low, large, thatched house was built for a meeting house and a school was also taught in the same building by Mrs. Hitchcock. As there was no law to compel attendance at school, at times there were many scholars, and again very few. People then seldom or never ventured into our house except on their hands and knees. We were called chiefs, which was not pleasant. Mr. Hitchcock and family would go to Kaunakakai, Halana, in small single canoes; to Wailau, Pelekunu and Kalaupapa in large ones, spend several days among the people and return by land over the pali, Mrs. H. being carried up by the natives, and Mr. H. and the children walking, unless the younger children were tired, when the natives would take them on their backs. Rev. Mr. and Mrs. Lowell Smith were sent as our associates in 1833. Mrs. Smith's health suffered there and they felt obliged to leave for medical advice before the end of the year, never returning again to stay. Much faithful labor for souls was done there by Mr. Hitchcock, and he was buried on Molokai as he promised the natives he would be. Rev. Mr. Forbes and family spent many years on Molokai after Mr. Hitchcock's death.

THE REVIVAL OF 1837 AT HILO, WITH PERSONAL RECOLLECTIONS.

BY DR. C. H. WETMORE.

"The story of the great work at Hilo" has been told so frequently and eloquently that it seems to me nearly, if not quite, presumptuous to attempt to repeat it to any audience except a youthful one, and such an audience should be gathered further away than this from the great scene of action. Allow me to weave into it some kindred topics in order to commend your attention and save weariness.

I will go back to the time when nine days after the brig "Thaddeus," laden with pioneer missionaries, had entered the Pacific Ocean. Just the day when that vessel turned her prow northward, aiming for their future home at these lovely islands, the cry of a little babe was heard, which assuaged a mother's sorrow as she was told that a man-child was born to her in a little town in Connecticut, celebrated for having been the home of the Trumbulls, the Buckinghams, and also, as having been the birth place of Dartmouth College. Little did that dear mother think of what would be the work or where would be the home of the child she that day caressed. For more than three score years has she, from her heavenly home, eagerly watched his career, although his long wanderings may have aroused her fears, yet she must have rejoiced with the angels of God when she beheld him choosing Jesus for his Savior and consecrating his powers to Him,—and later, too, when he was offering himself to the American Board of Foreign Missions to labor as a physician in some one or other of their dependencies. In this connection the father's name and influence must not be omitted; though not a great, he was a good man. It was his words, "Charles, think on these things," which, by the blessing of God, first turned the lad's thoughts to heavenly things in such a way as to result in his conversion; it was he too, who first whispered in his ear an encouraging word to enter eventually upon missionary toil.

It may interest you to know what providence God put in operation to send him in after years to live and labor here in the far west longitude, rather than in a land nearly twice as far away from home in an opposite direction.

In May, 1847, he and his intended wife had determined (deo volente) to respond to an imperative call from Madura. A debt for education intervened, but unexpectedly during the summer and autumn of that year, a way was opened for nearly cancelling the debt. Then a school had to be taught in order to open more fully the way for entering upon the anticipated labors. In the middle of winter he fixed upon a certain Saturday for visiting the Mission Rooms, at Pemberton Square, Boston. That week a very unruly boy in school needed discipline; in return he gave the teacher "a black eye," which unfitted him in appearance for the proposed visit. It was deferred two weeks. At the end of that period the contemplated trip was made, and great was his disappointment then to find that Dr. Shelton, of N. Y., (the husband of the lady who is now President of the Woman's Board), had received appointment, during that interval to the Madura mission. The choice then lay between Fuh Chau, West Africa, and the Sandwich Islands; in due time it was decided that the home should be here. Certainly, I hear you say, God often moves in mysterious ways, interweaving peculiar instrumentalities into his plans and purposes. Suffice to say, that after nearly a five months' voyage, via Cape Horn, in the ship "Leland," we saw at early dawn the summit of Mauna Kea, eighty miles distant, and the next morning we were warped into a safe place of anchorage in Honolulu harbor, not by a steam tug, but by a long string of natives, naked, save as to their "malos." It was Sabbath morning, Judge Lee and Hon. C. R. Bishop came on board with the pilot, and soon after Father Damon came off to tie the Judge's marriage knot; he (Father Damon) then kindly took us ashore; the first house we entered was the grand old Bethel, now in ashes. In the pulpit Father Dole was officiating for the tardy pastor. Before entering the house of God, we were introduced to a very influential member of the great reinforcement, viz: Father Castle, who drove up just at that time in an old-fashioned vehicle. After the services he took us home with him. When the Bethel meeting was over Mother Judd said, "As soon as I saw them I knew they were missionaries." The vessel bearing tidings of our appointment had a thirteen months' voyage, thus rendering our arrival a surprise to the entire mission circle.

The next thing I wish to allude to, is the weekly prayer meeting, held at Father Castle's. I was surprised to see such a large foreign assemblage gathered there to enjoy a meeting, with Father Armstrong as leader. I look back upon it to-day as a pleasant reminder of the past, and as one of the early leading features of the work here, helping, as it did, most efficiently in evangelizing the foreign elements, and in establishing and sustaining these thriving Christian institutions now in our midst.

In due time we were presented to King Kamehameha III. I was entirely unused to "court etiquette." When asked by His Majesty of my plans for the future, I said, "I expect to reside at the Islands." "WHAT *did you say?*" asked Mr. Wiley, *very gruffly.* I replied at the suggestion of one leaning on my arm, "With Your Majesty's permission," accompanying the same with a moderate bow, which quite relieved the old gentleman's mind, and put him in good humor again.

We arrived just in time to be present at that "General meeting," which discussed so energetically in the old mission school house certain resolutions, which came out from the home board fifty-two days ahead of us, via Mazatlan. The several resolutions received particular attention and soon modified the relations of several assistant missionaries to the special work in which they had enlisted. When the meeting was over we proceeded to our permanent earthly place of residence, feeling highly honored to be allowed to live and labor beside the Coans and Lymans. Years

have rolled by and *the five co-laborers* have been
called hence to a higher, holier work, while a lone
one yet remains at his post, awaiting a joyful reunion in bonds that know no isolation. Whilst
these changes have been going on, the same
mountains are still there in all their pristine
beauty and grandeur, and the same rivers flow as
ever into the mighty ocean. During this period
three new ones made their appearance. We thank
God that *He*, not Ruth Keliikalani, arrested their
molten streams and suffered them not to inundate
our homes, blot out our village, or obstruct our
safe and capacious harbor.

Father Lyman was the first to set me at work
at Hilo on the line of my profession; he also
mapped out for me other labors in his school-room,
thus affording an opportunity for acquiring the
language, with which I was anxious to become
familiar. Father Coan almost simultaneously
paved the way in a similar manner for my life
labors medically and surgically that he might the
more efficiently minister to his people the "Balm"
which is "in Gilead." It was my privilege early
to accompany Father Coan through Hilo district
on one of his quarterly preaching and school examination tours. Hilo was then densely populated. Travelling on foot, up, down, and through
those thirty ravines, or "canyons," and the numerous smaller ones, was very tedious to the uninitiated. Emerging from one of the former, the
eighth, on our first day, I expressed joy at being
over it. Two minutes later, as another came in
sight, with a third of still greater dimensions fol-

lowing it, Father Coan responded, "You must not rejoice too quickly!"—a lesson which I have since many a time learned to heed. During this and a subsequent tour through Puna, I witnessed his patient, persevering labors for his beloved flock. *Day, and much of the night,* he gave them in order to properly straighten up personal and church matters which had accumulated during the interval of pastoral visits. On one occasion, a little later, he acknowledged to another companion, that, after extending his work to a late hour in the night, he did *"feel a little leg weary."* Such expressions show that he was naturally jovial. He took with him a volume of "Rollin's Ancient History," which we read aloud whenever we had a few leisure moments. Trudging along, we discussed many interesting and important topics; some of them I well remember; one or two of them must suffice. "In man and animals where is the line of demarkation between reason and instinct, and what really is instinct?" Again, "The longevity of man, will it not eventually be much greater than it now is, if men will only learn to properly control their appetites and passions?" We would get up considerable excitement over them and then conclude that after all we did not know much about such matters.

The Sabbath school celebrations followed by general feasting were noteworthy objects connected with those summer and autumn tours. Father Coan's youthful days occurred during the 1812 war-period. Although he was a strong peace man, he evidently imbibed many elementary tac-

tics from those military surroundings. Sabbath
school children and older persons caught from
him the spirit of those evolutions, which he made
with such regularity and celerity. His presence
seemed to infuse life into all their proceedings.
They appeared quite satisfied in those days when
their acts met his unqualified approval. Churches,
as you all well know, were then large, and required
patient and faithful attention to keep them in
good working condition. The incipient prelimin-
ary work, which brought these extraordinary
churches into existence, my eyes did not behold.
I did, however, often sit and listen attentively to
Father Coan's and Father Lyman's report of those
golden days. Before devoting any special attention to them, it will be quite appropriate for us to
first turn backward a leaf or two of history. Let
me allude to what Father Lyman once told me of
the early days of Christianity here. He said that
at times there were fears that the people would
lapse again into idolatry; especially was it so
when the beloved Kaahumanu died nineteen days
after their arrival. At first the people generally
thought that with her death the schools would
cease to exist, and the "pono" die too. It took
time to correct that impression and to convince
them (particularly those whose apparent religious-
ness arose from the influence of the chiefs,) that
God still lived and regarded them with the same
favor he ever had done. It was very gratifying
to me to hear him talk about that noble Christian
woman. That although she was naturally "proud,
haughty, selfish and oppressive," traits of charac-

ter directly opposite to these were developed in her, so much so that when she visited Hilo on that remarkable general tour of her's, to recommend religion and encourage schools, the Hilo people called her "the new Kaahumanu." He spoke of her great influence over Hawaiians. A heathen woman converted late in life, she did not live or die in vain, resting from her labors her works followed her.

The venerable missionary fathers and mothers at Hilo delighted in rehearsing the revival scenes and work of 1837–8. They told me of the multitudes who gathered about their houses and elsewhere for instruction and human help after the Holy Spirit had arrested their attention and made them feel that they were sinners and in perishing need of saving mercy. Their hands were full as they pointed men, women and children to "the Lamb of God, which taketh away the sin of the world." Time was hardly allowed them for taking their proper meals, or, for giving "tired nature's sweet restorer" opportunity to do its wonted work. At Puna, Father Coan pointed out to me the place where *he* first noticed the commencement of the Pentacostal season, and how it there resulted in real conversions. Very soon after this a general awakening occurred in both Puna and Hilo. Protracted meetings were held as in other countries when in similar circumstances. Inquirers came fifty or sixty miles to participate in them; great numbers kept on seeking until they found the blessings so much desired. Finally the time came to open the church doors and receive to its bosom the hundreds of converts, who were the fruits of that precious revival. Father Coan assured me that that work was done carefully and prayerfully ; 1,705 in July, 450 in October, 786 in November, 357 in December, and 1,946 at other communion seasons, were gathered into the Hilo fold, making the entire number 5,244 in one year. All of them had been previously subjected to what was considered a proper season of probation, quite as long as is usual in Christian countries. Surely the blessing of God did, as in apostolic times, rest on their arduous labors; in the morning they sowed the seed. and at evening they withheld not their hands.

It was about a dozen years after this wonderful out-pouring of God's Spirit, when I took up my residence among them. I can only speak personally of those days and their sequels. Measles had just decimated their number and many had passed away with a sure and steadfast hope-anchor. Aged, middle-aged and youthful, Christians were living on, a great many of whom, though so recently having emerged from the midnight darkness of paganism, continued to "walk worthy of their high vocation," and were regarded by all of us as stable Christians. Having previously watched Christian efforts in four different States of the Union, I was the better prepared to judge of its development here. When I saw those men and women meeting so often and so regularly for the study of God's word, and heard their voices pleading so earnestly, and with such child-like simplicity for God's blessing, not only upon themselves, but upon mankind the world over, I was constrained to exclaim; *"Behold, what hath God here wrought?"* At that time the old "Haili" Church edifice was in existence, and lasted an entire decade of years. The thatching would rot, the roof would leak. Stated days had to be fixed for patching or rethatching that vast building; companies were detailed here and there to gather the varied materials for this object. Although "po ulua" and "konohiki" days often caused interruptions and delay in the Lord's work, yet they would persevere in it until leakage and decay were arrested and the house made comfortable for religious worship. Time spent upon objects of this nature told for good among our Christian population as well as upon those who were not numbered with the disciples. A score of years I attended quite regularly the "Haili" Church. At every communion season, from 1849 to 1869, additions were made to that Christian household.

Three days before we left Boston a rumor reached the "Hub of the universe," that gold had been discovered in California; the report needed confirmation before it could be generally believed. About the time we crossed the equator in this ocean a vessel hove in sight and gave us a "Friend," which told the whole story, announcing the rush thither from Hawaii nei and elsewhere. This after a time changed greatly the state of things temporally and spiritually. Money soon became more commonly the circulating medium. The wants of the people increased. Not long after this more costly and more desirable dwelling houses, school houses and church buildings were in demand. All these things tended more or less to divert the minds of the people from religious to secular matters. Yet facts show that a large number of them held fast their profession, giving good evidence that they had, indeed, passed from death into life.

It was intensely interesting in those earlier days to see Christians keep with them at home and abroad their "ai-o-ka-la" (daily food), and their hymn book, and to hear them day by day repeat over and over again (whole families of them) the passage of Scripture specially designated, that they might thoroughly commit it to memory as a portion of their Sabbath school exercises, and then strive to learn its meaning and the lesson it taught. The present and the rising generation would do well to learn lessons from, and pattern after, such predecessors; it is to be feared that they have nearly forgotten them and those halcyon days. Retrograde, or at least down hill, steps, where once entered upon are much more easily taken than those in the opposite direction. Deaf ears and obdurate hearts are very difficult to be reached after the great enemy of souls once gets them under his influence and control. Thank God! there is a mightier power, which can gain possession of such minds and hearts too, when He sees best to send forth that "still, small voice," which for so many centuries has been doing its efficient, saving work. We need not therefore despair, even if there are very dark days before us, and the floodgates of sin are wide open all around us. I have spoken of school houses, Let me here say, it was a dark period for us immediately after those flames were extinguished, which left the "Hilo Boarding School" buildings of 1853 in embers. But a fresh and deeper interest in such objects succeeded it. We can now point to a group of new buildings, made of less inflammable materials, where pupils are still gathered for instruction. and from which salutary and elevating influences annually go forth. It is a very gratifying fact that the "Lyman Fund" of ten thousand dollars, devised by Rev. W. B. Oleson, has at last been fully completed. In this connection, (after mentioning the munificence of Hon. C. R. Bishop for this object,) it is a matter worthy of note that in addition to it, the sum of one thousand, four hundred and twenty-five dollars, (which is one-seventh of the entire Fund,) has been donated by the members and their families of that "strong reinforcement," whose semi-centennial we to-day celebrate and commemorate. They also gave more than one-fifth of the amount raised by private subscriptions for the new "industrial building," now being constructed.

At this late era we can review the past and see that evangelization and civilization have moved on hand in hand in accomplishing the great work, which emanated from those tears, which Opukahaia shed so profusely "upon the threshold of Yale College." This grand work progressed at times quite moderately, and then again, with very rapid strides. One example will serve as an elucidation of this subject. When our people decided to build a new house of worship all Hilo and Puna gave as the Lord prospered them towards attaining this desirable object. Those who lived in our immediate vicinity spent much time in collecting stone for its walls, which were afterwards used simply for the foundation. Scarcely anyone came to the Wednesday or Saturday afternoon meetings without an offering in this line. As the years passed away both the stores and the funds increased until the present durable and commodious house took the place of their old one, as the Jewish temple of olden times displaced the Tabernacle, which they had so long venerated. Not long after this the new regime of 1863 went into operation. Then our natives had but little money to raise towards sustaining their Gospel institutions. And now, while we have church edifices sufficiently numerous, and enough young men being educated for the ministry in our " North Pacific Missionary Institute " to occupy them, few of these ministers can obtain a decent livelihood, the people having forgotten the ancient instruction, " Thou shalt not muzzle the ox that treadeth out the corn." The time for the American Board to " withdraw their care from the Islands and leave them to themselves" was not as near at hand as they supposed when they sent out their great 1873 re-enforcement. In 1863, too, it was further off in the future than we, at that time, supposed. The change then made worked well for a time, but results indicate that if those steps had been deferred a score of years, it would have been much more salutary to the churches and to the people themselves.

While we to-day dwell largely upon the work accomplished by that company now represented here by six of the original members, and bless God that He put it into their hearts thus to come and live and labor here in whatever capacity they were needed, let us also remember that there is much yet to be done ; that they, their descendants, and all of us bearing the Christian name, residing in this realm, must follow up these efforts, striving with all our personal energy to make vast achievements for the beloved Master in the future, so that there shall continue to be great joy among celestial and terrestrial inhabitants over penitent ones all about us, who have turned their eager footsteps through the "wicket gate," Zionward.

Evidently the great want of this age is the presence of the re-vivifying Spirit of God. It should be our united prayer that it revisit us with the same saving efficacy that was witnessed here when that company of thirty-two missionaries, from eight different States of the Union, received appointment to come to the sunny islands to put on and here wear the missionary harness. Finally it would be well for the "American Board" to reconsider what they have done in years gone by, and, if possible, take back in their own hands some of the good work which they have relinquished, and so strive to regain their former attitude in relation to the churches, which they have been instrumental in planting, and which were for so long a time under their fostering care. Let this be done, and, with God's blessing upon us, the Christian world may, with more potency, continue to appoint men hitherward to note what missionary work can effect, and has effected in what was once a pagan country.

---o---

FOUR YEARS OF MISSION WORK, 1833-37.

BY REV. LOWELL SMITH.

The 5th reinforcement of the Sandwich Islands Mission consisted of Rev. B. W. Parker and wife, and Rev. Lowell Smith and wife. We arrived at Honolulu on the first day of May, 1833, some four years previous to the 7th reinforcement, whose Jubilee we have met to celebrate on this occasion.

The annual meeting of the mission that year, 1833, was held in June, at Lahaina. During that meeting, the subject of establishing a mission at the Marquesas Islands, where a committee had previously been sent to spy out the land, was fully discussed, and decided in the affirmative. Messrs. Alexander, Armstrong and Parker and their wives, were the successful candidates for said mission. It was also voted that Brother and Sister Tinker be associated with Brother Green at Wailuku; and that Mrs. Smith and myself be located at Kaluaaha, on Molokai, as associates with Mr. and Mrs. Hitchcock. On arriving at the station, we found that much had been done in preparing the way of the Lord on that Island. A school house and meeting house were ready for use, our associates had acquired language enough to commence keeping school and holding meetings on the Sabbath.

Lazarus, the principal chief at the station, presented us with a small grass house, with a lauhala mat for a floor, and the same material for a door and window. But unfortunately for us, the house leaked badly every time it rained; Mrs. Smith took cold, and by over work in her domestic duties, broke down in health, and was quite an invalid for several years.

Our first business, of course, was to learn the language. In this we were greatly favored in finding the New Testament translated; and also a number of elementary school books ready for use.

The first Sabbath after our arrival, several hundred people assembled in their new meeting house. Brother Hitchcock preached to them in the morning, and in the afternoon, I held forth in English, and Brother Hitchcock interpreted for me.

Not being satisfied with our grass house, and there being an old heiau, or pile of good stones near by, I resolved to build a stone house, using common mud for mortar. Having been brought up on a farm, I felt assured I could make a door and window better suited to keep out rogues, dogs and pigs, than a lauhala mat· So I employed natives to go into the mountains for plates, beams and rafters; and others to bring stones and help lay up the walls of the house; and while the work was going on, I learned to say, "hele mai," "hele aku," "lawe mai," "lawe aku." "hapai," "hana pono." "hana paa," etc., etc.

I also commenced a singing school, in which the scholars helped me in my pronunciation of the language, while I was training their voices to sing.

In due time my stone house was finished, with a good thatched roof; a batten door hung on hinges, and a glass window for light and ventilation. This at the time was regarded as quite a step forward in civilization.

In the course of three months I wrote a sermon, and read it over to Brother Hitchcock for his criticism. Then rewrote it with additions and subtractions, according to his suggestions. Then read it over to him again. Now, said he, next Sabbath you must read that to the congregation. Yes, said I, but you must perform the devotional exercises. At noon, during the Sabbath school, Brother Hitchcock questioned the scholars to see if they understood any part of the sermon. Several of them repeated the text, and some of them the heads of the discourse, which was quite gratifying to me.

Daily morning prayer meetings were held at the station, and were well attended by the people in that neighborhood, and it was obvious to us that the Holy Spirit was in the midst of us, convincing some of their sins and ill deserts.

Having come from a land of protracted meetings and powerful revivals, we proposed to invite

Brother Richards, Spaulding and Tinker, to come over from Lahaina and help us in a meeting of two or three days. The natives gave good attention to the sermons preached by the brethren, and we all felt that the Spirit of God was with us on that occasion. But this was only a forerunner of the great and powerful protracted meetings held all over the Islands in the near future.

During the year I wrote and preached some sixteen or eighteen sermons, talked and prayed more or less in the morning prayer meetings and monthly concerts, and I began to feel quite at home in the Hawaiian dialect.

GENERAL MEETING, 1834.

The general meeting this year was held in June, at Honolulu.

On arriving there we were surprised to learn that the Marquesan Mission was abandoned, and the brethren had all returned to Honolulu. But in due time they gave their reasons for so doing, and were received back again as members of the Hawaiian Mission.

One of the subjects for discussion during the meeting was, whether it was better for two clerical brethren to be located together, or each family have a separate station ? The latter opinion prevailed. The locating committee then recommended that Brother Alexander be located at Hanalei, on Kauai; Brother Armstrong at Hamakua, on Maui; Brother Parker at Kaneohe, on Oahu; and that Mrs. Smith and myself be removed from Molokai to the district of Ewa on this Island.

According to the recent census, there were about five thousand people in the district, including Waianae as an out station. The people were scattered along in thirteen small villages or ahupuaa upon the coast from Halawa to Honouliuli— and thence on to Waianae, some twenty miles. Formerly, under the mandate of the chiefs; if notice was previously given that Brother Clark, or some other missionary would come and preach on the Sabbath, a thousand people, more or less, would assemble to-gether.

But a *revolution backward* had just taken place; and the moral aspect was quite dark and discouraging.

The young Prince, Kauikeouli, subsequently Kamehameha III; whose headquarters for dissipation were at Waipio—had recently plunged into a debauch of intemperance and licentiousness; and the *hula* was in full blast all through the district; the great majority of the people had forsaken the pono, and were following in the wake of the Prince. It was several months before I could get more than one hundred and fifty people together on the Sabbath.

Mrs. Smith being in feeble health, remained at Honolulu, until I could build a house suitable for us to live in. In the mean time, I preached at the station every Sabbath; organized a Sabbath school; attended one or two district meetings during the week, and did what I could for the sick and dying in the neighborhood. But we did not move into our new house and get settled, till the *15th of November*.

Soon after this, I commenced a common school among the children at the station; a singing school among the adults; and a regular Sabbath morning prayer meeting. The people then took it for granted, that the missionaries had come *to stay*, and soon began to favor us with presents of fowls, pigs, taro, potatoes, bananas, etc.

Several good praying men and women, members of the Church at Honolulu, lived at Waiawa, and were a great comfort to us; and did much to stay up our hands, while we were calling for the Holy Spirit to descend and aid us in winning souls to Christ. From this time forth, my Sabbath congregations gradually increased. There was a great deal of sickness among the people, and I spent much time in visiting among them. My success as a physician induced many to forsake their native doctors, and to attend public worship on the Sabbath.

In January, 1835, I made a tour to Waianae, in company with Punahaole, a good man, where we met Brother Emerson and Kuokoa, his right hand man. But the *revolution backward* at Waianae was worse if possible than it had been at Ewa. We found it very difficult to get more than twenty-five or thirty persons together to a religious meeting. We spent one night there talking with Madam Boki and Kaapuiki and a few others, trying to persuade them to forsake their evil ways and accept of salvation as it is offered in the Gospel. People who have been partially Christianized, and then turn back again to folly and heathenism, are apparently far worse than ever.

On our way to Waianae, we saw a heathen God by the side of the road. It was a stone dressed with tapa, standing upon a pile of stones. Its worshipers offerred it a piece of tapa every time they passed by it. Alas for those whose gods are naught but wood and stone.

But thanks to the Lord, the prospects at the central station are brightening every Sabbath.

The last week in march I accompanied Brother Tinker to Waialua to assist Brother Emerson in a protracted meeting among his people. We preached three sermons a day, besides a morning and evening prayer meeting. The audience was attentive and solemn after a season of probation, a number were received to the Church as the fruits of that meeting.

Being encouraged by the meeting at Waialua, I appointed a protracted meeting at Ewa, to commence on the 15th of April, and invited Messrs. Bingham, Tinker and Emerson to come and assist me. During the week previous to the meeting, the natives prepared an extra amount of food, both for themselves and others, who might come to the meeting. Brother Emerson came on at the appointed time, followed by forty of his people, and Brother Tinker was preceded by about thirty Church membars from Honolulu. And to my surprise, not less than five hundred came in from the different lands from Halawa all along to Honouliuli, and we soon felt that the Spirit of God was in the midst of us.

We requested the Church members to improve every opportunity to hold prayer meetings among themselves; and also invite the impenitent to come with them to hear the sermons. Brother Tinker and Emerson alternated in preaching till Friday noon, when Brother Tinker left, and Brother Bingham came and labored with us till after the Sabbath.

It was very obvious that the master who said, "Go preach my Gospel, and lo, I am with you," was there verifying his promise. The protracted meeting closed Monday forenoon; but the daily morning prayer meetings were continued, and many came to talk with us, confessing their sins, and expressing hope in Christ for their salvation.

GENERAL MEETING, 1835.

The mission families looked forward to the annual meetings in June with a good deal of interest. Having been isolated for ten or twelve months, seldom seeing anyone but natives, it was a great comfort to meet once a year and spend three or four weeks together, talking over their labors, trials, joys and sorrows in their missionary work. But the long, tedious voyages to and fro in the small native schooners of 1834-5 were very different from the quick, pleasant voyages of 1887 in our large island steamers.

The general meeting 1835 was organized on the 4th day of June. And on the 6th, the ship Helespont arrived with the annual supplies of the mission, from Boston, with the 6th reinforcement of missionaries, eight in number, viz: Rev. Titus Coan and wife, Mr. E. O. Hall and wife, Mr. H. Dimond and wife, Miss Lydia Brown, and Miss Elizabeth M. Hitchcock.

Brother Coan and wife were located at Hilo, where they lived, labored and died in the cause of their Lord and Master. Messrs. Hall and Dimond were located in Honolulu as printer and book-binder for the Mission. Miss Brown, who came to teach the natives how to spin cotton, and make it into cloth, cut it into garments, knit stockings, etc., was located first at Wailuku, on Maui, and afterwards on Molokai. Miss Hitchcock was associated with her brother and his wife at Kaluaaha, on Molokai, but subsequently married Mr. E. H. Rogers, the printer.

All the members of this reinforcement are dead and gone, except Mr. and Mrs. Dimond.

The 18th of June was observed as a day of fasting, humiliation and prayer, in view of the low state of religion, and the few conversions at the missionary stations the year past. Brother Coan and others addressed the families several times, and something like a revival took place among the larger children. This put new life and hope in all the brethren for the future.

TRIP TO KAUAI AND BACK.

On the 2d of July, 1835, at the close of general meeting, I accompanied Messrs. Whitney and Gulick and their families to Waimea, Kauai, on the schooner Palua. This was my first voyage and visit to that island. With the regular trade winds, sailing vessels run down to Kauai in one night. We left with a fair wind at 2 P. M., but before sundown we were becalmed off Waianae, and lay there rolling and tumbling all night. Next morning a head wind set us in motion, and at 9 o'clock it commenced raining with a strong breeze, which lasted us all day. About sundown we discovered Kauai, and about dark came under the lee of the island; the wind and rain abating, we sailed pleasantly along the southwest side of the island and at midnight were off Waimea. The moon having gone down, it was too dark to go on shore; so we stood off and on till morning, then entered the harbor and dropped anchor at 6 e'clock. Natives came off with canoes and carried us ashore, and at nine o'clock we took breakfast at Brother Whitney's. I was pretty well pleased with the conveniences at Waimea station. There were two good framed houses for the mission families; a good stone meeting house 90 by 40 feet., plastered inside and out; and a very easy house to speak in, compared with the grass houses on Oahu.

But by the vote of the Mission, last year, Brother Gulick and family were removed from Waimea to Koloa, 15 miles to the windward. On Saturday, Brother Gulick and family left for Koloa on the Palua, and I remained and preached for Brother Whitney. Monday morning, I left for Koloa on horseback, and arrived there about 8 o'clock.

Koloa station is about a mile from the shore, and commands a fine prospect mai-o-a-o. I was much pleased with Brother Gulick's new station.

The Palua sailed from Koloa Monday noon for Oahu, which made my visit at Koloa very short. Tuesday evening we were under the lee of Waianae again, but bound to Waialua, where I landed next morning at 9 o'clock, and took Brother Emerson by surprise! There I borrowed a horse and crossed over the plain that afternoon to Ewa, and took the people there by surprise; employed a couple of men to row my canoe that night at high tide to Honolulu; and the next morning took Mrs. Smith and the families at Honolulu by surprise. They said they thought that I had gone to Kauai. And as the Palua had not returned, they did not understand how I should be in Honolulu.

SECOND YEAR AT EWA.

We were much encouraged during the second year of our residence and labors at Ewa, in the steady increase of the congregation on the Sabbuth, and the district schools during the week; and the satisfactory evidence that twelve or thirteen persons had become true Christians.

On Saturday the 15th of August, I made another visit to Waianae, and spent the Sabbath there; accompanied by some of the Hawaiian brethren from Ewa; and we were very kindly and hospitably entertained by Kaapuiki, the head man of the district. This time he not only gave us enough to eat and drink, but he presented us a new house, well furnished with mats and sleeping tapa, which he said was for the use of the teacher and his attendants whenever he came to Waianae.

At the blowing of the horn Saturday evening, 127 natives came to our meeting. At sunrise, Sabbath morning, 150 came; and at 10 A. M., we
8

had an audience of 257. At the prayer meeting, Monday morning, 150 came ; and at the close, *seven couple presented themselves to be married !!* This was obviously turning over a new leaf. We returned to Ewa that day, quite encouraged for the district of Waianae.

In October, Brother Parker invited his missionary brethren to come and aid him in a protracted meeting at Kaneohe. Such meetings were becoming quite popular on Oahu ; and not only church members, but the hoikaikas were anxious to accompany the missionaries to those meetings. Nearly one hundred followed Brother Emerson from Waialua and Kolauloa ; and nearly as many went over from Ewa and Honolulu. The Kaneohe people were quite surprised at the number of visitors ; but regarding it as a pentacostal season, opened their doors and had all things common for six days and nights. The average congregation was about six hundred, but Sabbath morning it increased to a thousand. It was a good meeting, and I leave it for Mrs. Parker to tell us the fruits thereof.

CHURCH ORGANIZATION.

The Church at Ewa was organized on the Sabbath, January 3d, 1836. Messrs. Bingham and Emerson were with us, and officiated on that solemn occasion. *Six* persons were received by letter from the Church at Kawaiahao ; and *twelve* on profession of their faith in Christ, as a part of the fruit of our protracted meeting the year before ; a little church of 18 members at its organization, but which subsequently numbered more than 2,800.

NEW MEETING HOUSE.

Being in need of a new house of worship at Ewa, I cast about to see where we could get materials suitable for the walls of the house. There was no heiau at Ewa, nor quarry of stones, as at some of the othes stations. There were no lumber yards in Honolulu, where lumber could be obtained for such a building. But I ascertained that the soil there would make good strong adobies. if well mixed with manienie grass. And the natives were ready to do anything in their power to accomplish the desired object. So I told them that some of the men could make the adobies and assist the mason in laying up the walls of the house; and other men could go into the mountains and get timbers for the plates— beams—rafters, and also for the roof; and the women could make taula for thatching the roof, and lauhala mats for the flooring.

I also ascertained that Brindsmade, Ladd & Co., merchants of Honolulu, had a great demand from whale ships for *potatoes, taro, fowls, pigs, goats, turkies, bananas and fire wood,* for all of which if delivered at Honolulu, they would take and pay us out of their store in boxes of glass, kegs of nails, cotton cloth, etc.

The natives replied, that they could contribute more or less of these articles; and that those who were *hemahema* could go to the woods and get firewood; and that they would carry the contributions to Honolulu in their canoes. The way being prepared, the natives commenced in good earnest to bring in their gifts for the new meeting house. The first month we realized $18.00, (i. e.) three boxes of glass. The second, $27.50, for which we got a box of glass and a keg of nails. The third month, $38.00, $7.50 of which was cash. The people at Waialua heard what we were doing and they sent us a monthly contribution, for which we realized about $40.00. By and by our Molokai friends sent us a lot of turkies and fowls, pigs and taro, for which we realized $35.00. Some of our benevolent friends in Honolulu presented us a few *dollars in cash;* and we were fully assured that in due time, we should have the means of building a nice large adobe meeting house at Ewa.

HOIKE OF SCHOOLS.

On the 25th of May, 1836, we had a *hoike*, or examination of the district schools. Both teachers and scholars appeared much better than at any former examination. The grand defect in most of the teachers is the want of ability to govern and keep order.—Aole hiki ke hoomalu i na haumana. Having never been taught to properly obey their own parents, the children were very noisy and ungovernable in school.

At our examination in 1835, only 175 came together. But this time there were 522. On the whole, we were quite encouraged at the change for the better, both in the common schools and the Sabbath school; the large and steady increase of the congregation, the organization of a church of eighteen members, and of the prospect of being able soon to build a nice large house of worship.

I ought perhaps to state that Mrs. Smith was an invalid these two years, and not able to labor much among the women in prayer meeting, or in teaching school, which was her favorite employment in after years. Dr. Judd made her many visits during our residence at Ewa.

GENERAL MEETING, JUNE, 1836.

When the Locating Committee was appointed, Dr. Judd enquired if some arrangement could not be made to have Mrs. Smith located, for a time, at Honolulu, on account of her ill health.

The Committee cast about and learned that Mrs. Bishop was anxious to remove from Kailua to some station where she could have exercise in cultivating a garden. The station at Ewa was just such a place, good rich soil, and near a splendid spring of water.

Some of the brethren said there were a host of children and youth in Honolulu who ought to be in a good school, and that some brother ought to be set apart to that work; and to accommodate the two sisters, they would recommend that Mr. and Mrs. Smith come to Honolulu for a year, more or less, and do what they can for the children and youth; and that Mr. and Mrs. Bishop remove to Ewa, pro tem, and engage in the missionary work there. and superintend the building of the new church.

It made our *hearts ache* to think of leaving Ewa; but all things considered, together with the wish and unanimous vote of the mission, we consented to the arrangement. It seemed to us like following in the footsteps of our Lord and Master, who went about doing good, but had no certain dwelling place.

SCHOOL KEEPING.

There were two school houses at Kawaiahao; one in the yard where the Female Seminary is located; this was called Dr. Judd's school house; this was for the boys. The other was makai of the stone church where the mission families held their general meetings; this was for the girls.

On the 8th of July, the horn was blown, and thirty-five boys came to the mauka school house —*eleven* of whom did not know the alphabet. I commenced with two native assistant teachers; a man and woman. I told them that the native schools are generally very noisy and disobedient; but in this school we must have order; and, said I, we will commence the school with prayer to our Lord and Master, who commanded his disciples to go and preach the Gospel to the poor and ignorant, and said, "lo I am with you unto the end of the world." And He also said unto them, "without me ye can do nothing." I wish you all to know that "the fear of the Lord is the beginning of wisdom." On the 14th the horn was blown to call the girls together, and fifty-nine came; and they were as noisy and kolohe as you can well imagine. I called them to order, and opened the school with prayer. I assured them that we must have order and quiet, if they wish to learn their lessons. Many of them were in their *teens;* but having never been trained to obey their parents they were slow to submit to the rules of my school. I proposed to have two schools in operation, both morning and afternoon, and I would superintend them both. The assistant teachers kept good order when I was present, but during my absence the children were very noisy and disobedient.

I told both schools that I proposed to hold two religious meetings with them every Sabbath—the first at 8 o'clock A. M., in the meeting house; and the second at the school house at 2 P. M., and that their parents and friends could come too if they wished to.

Sabbath morning, July 24th, at the blowing of the horn, three hundred and fifty persons assembled in the meeting house, and behaved very well. At 2 P. M., some two hundred met me in the school house. I gave them fully to understand what I purposed to do, both as a teacher, and a preacher of the gospel. The next day one hundred and three boys and one hundred and twenty-four girls came to school. I at once saw that the harvest was great, and the laborers few; and immediately appointed more teachers in both schools.

I also commenced an evening singing school among the adults, to train a few voices to aid in public worship on the Sabbath.

We kept a record of all the names of the scholars the first term, and there were enrolled 226 girls, and 166 boys—392 in all. But only 125 girls and 80 boys had attended regularly. There had been very little seriousness manifested in the schools; but on the whole we thought our labor had not been in vain.

OCTOBER 20TH VACATION.

Brother Parker and myself, and our wives, feeling the need of a change, we made arrangements with Hopili, whose schooner was bound to the windward, to take us as passengers to Kaluaaha, on Molokai, and drop anchor and wait for us until after the Sabbath; and then take us to Kahului, on Maui, and there leave us to take care of ourselves. We had a pleasant visit with Brother and Sister Hitchcock—preached to his congregation on the Sahbath, and on Tuesday took anchor and sailed for Kahului, and dropped anchor there next morning at 9 o'clock; and took the families at Wailuku, Messrs. Green and Armstrong, by surprise. They regarded our visit there at that time as very providential; for they had appointed a protracted meeting to commence on the 1st of November, and we must prolong our visit, and assist them in the meeting. We consented so to do. The audience was large—not less than one thousand people assembled at the first morning prayer meeting. The Holy Spirit accompanied the word preached from day to day, and several persons were hopefully converted.

Our next move was for Lahainaluna, to assist the teachers in a protracted meeting with their scholars. At Maalaea Bay we took passage on canoes to Lahaina, and thence by land to the school. We had an interesting meeting with those young men, from Thursday morning till Sabbath evening. They gave good attention, and several expressed penitence for sin and faith in the Lord Jesus Christ.

November 14th, we took passage on board the Charles Carrol, Capt. Weeks, who gave us a free passage. At 7 P M., dropped anchor in the outer harbor. The next morning the captain took us ashore in his boat.

SCHOOL AGAIN.

On the 21st of November, called my two schools together again. The first day 110 girls and 50 boys. Some of the boys were sick, and others had gone to Koolau, but the average number was soon made up to over 200.

December 26, 1836, news arrived from Boston about the 7th reinforcement. Dr. Anderson informed us that the Prudential Committee had appointed three clergymen, two physicians, nine school masters, one secular agent and their wives, and two single ladies for this mission, who may arrive here in April or May, 1837. This was good news and glad tidings, for the field was white and already for the harvest.

At New Year, 1837, it was announced that there were to be four protracted meetings on Oahu, of five or six days each, in the following order:

1st, at Kawaiahao, to commence January 31st;
2d, at Ewa, to commence February 15th;
3rd, at Waialua, to commence March 8th;

8*

4th, at Kaneohe, to commence April 1st.

Several of my scholars were hopefully converted during these meeting. They were glorious meetings; a kind of pentacostal season at each of the stations; and the commencement of the great revival, which spread all over the Islands, and continued for three years. Not less than 50,000 persons were received into the churches, as the fruits of that revival and its subsequent labors.

And will it not be well for the grand children of this association to add this as an important supplement to the records of this Jubilee?

Here also is another paragraph which might be added, unless some of the 7th Reinforcement have embodied the same in their communications.

On the arrival of the bark Mary Frazier, the missionaries assured us that they had a precious revival of religion on board during their passage; that Capt. Sumner, his second mate, and four of the sailors had become praying Christians. And about two weeks after their arrival, at their own request, Brother Bingham received them into the Kawaiahao Church.

SCHOOL EXAMINATION.

On the 19th of April, we had another examination of all the district schools of Honolulu. Some twelve or thirteen hundred all told. Of my two schools, two hundred and twenty-four were present, and appeared well. The most of them had made commendable improvement in their studies, such as reading, writing, geography and arithmetic.

We felt quite encouraged to go forward from the fact, that not only the missionaries, but the chiefs and parents of the children, expressed a deep interest in the progress of the scholars of my schools.

By special request I selected *four* of the most promising boys to go to Lahainaluna, viz: Kapeau, Kaiawa, Keaka and Kamakea.

GENERAL MEETING, MAY, 1837.

Most of the mission families having arrived at Honolulu. the General Meeting was organized on the 3rd of May.

The location of the 7th Reinforcement being a subject of deep interest to us all; a committee of location was early appointed. And after mature deliberation and consultation, they presented the following report, which was adopted:

On Kauai.—Dr. and Mrs. Lafon be located at Koloa; Mr. and Mrs. Johnson at Waioli.

On Oahu.—Mr. and Mrs. Cooke, Mr. and Mrs. Castle at Honolulu; Miss Marcia M. Smith at Punahou; Mr. and Mrs. Locke at Waialua.

On Molokai. | Mr. and Mrs. Munn at Kaluaaha.

On Maui.—Mr. and Mrs. Ives (pro tem) at Lahaina; Miss Lucia G. Smith at Lahainaluna; Mr. and Mrs Conde, Mr. and Mrs. McDonald at Hana.

On Hawaii.—Mr. and Mrs. Bliss, Mr. and Mrs. Bailey at Kohala; Dr. and Mrs. Andrews at Waimea; Mr. and Mrs. Wilcox at Hilo; Mr. and Mrs. Van Duzee at Kailua; Mr. and Mrs. Knapp at Kaawaloa.

Supplement.—That Mr. and Mrs. Bishop remain at Ewa, and that Mr. and Mrs. Lowell Smith take a new station. at Kaumakapili.

February 20th, 1837—Mrs. Dibble died at Lahainaluna.

May 14th, 1837—Mrs. Lyons died at Honolulu, during General Meeting.

I will simply add that I continued to superintend those schools till the quarterly examination in October, when two hundred and fifty-five of my pupils were present and appeared well. Messrs. Andrews, Bingham, Chamberlain Judd and. Hall were present, and also several of the ladies. *I then and there resigned* my office as school master at Kawaiahao; and Mr. and Mrs. Cooke were appointed as my successors. Mrs. Cooke being present, can tell you the sequel of that school.

I have thus far spoken freely of my experiences and work, in accordance with the circular sent me some months ago.

I will now give place for the survivors of the 7th Reinforcement to speak as freely of their experiences and work.

———o———

RECOLLECTIONS OF THE HAWAIIAN MISSION AND ITS SEVENTH REINFORCEMENT.

BY SERENO E. BISHOP.

Being almost the only one one present of the children of the missionaries living here in the year 1837, and then old enough to retain distinct memories of that time, may I be pardoned the apparent egotism of introducing personal circumstances and reminiscences into this paper.

The powerful reinforcement of our Mission in 1837, by the large company of thirty-two persons on the Mary Frazier forms a very marked point in my memories of the old Mission days. It was both the largest company of missionaries, and the largest company of white passengers that had ever come to Honolulu, and naturally created a great sensation among all classes of people here. Once before, in 1832, a reinforcement of nineteen persons had arrived by the Averick. I have a quite well-defined recollection of the appearance of those young men and women as they sat in Mrs. Bingham's parlor in the old Mission house the day that they landed. I have seen several of their great-grandchildren, though I remember some of their faces as then strangely blooming and youthful. For I had never before seen a fresh, young white woman's face. Those Averick men are all gone home; a minority of the women still survive in a good old age. They made a magnificent record of fruitful work for Christ and souls, and Hawaiian progress. Rev. Messrs. Smith, Parker and Coan had subsequently joined the Mission, as well as Messrs. Hall and Dimond, who imparted great impetus to the work of publication. The older missionaries were in their full prime of vigor and experience, while the younger men were becoming veterans in the work, all forming a united and goodly corps of Christian soldiers as I well remember them, full of loving zeal, of efficient and fruitful labors, and of a peculiarly enthusiastic faith, which was justified by the wonderful progress already made, and which I was already old enough to appreciate and admire.

The power and promise of the Gospel work had so grown—the ripening harvest seemed so copious—that in answer to the large and urgent demands of this Mission, the American Board responded by gathering and sending out to their help this large force of four ordained missionaries, one physician, and ten teachers, with their wives, and two single ladies. I well remember the thrill of wonder and enthusiasm in my childish mind at the news which arrived that a "reinforcement" (familiar word) of thirty-two "new missionaries" was on the way. It seemed to mean everything that was good, new society, new ideas, new pushing of good things, every wonderful and delightful interest—and it was all incomparably more than realized.

The Bishops had the year before left our old home near the Thurstons at Kailua, and were then living at Ewa, whence Lowell Smith had gone to take charge of the school system in Honolulu, shortly after to establish the parish of Kaumakapili. He used to make very frequent visits to us in his old parish, with tne tails of his clawhammer coat carefully pinned in a diagonal fold, away from contact with his horse's back. I think I had then seen no other form of coat except jackets, which our fathers often wore about the house. We were at that time just finishing the great adobe church, whose dimensions proved too small for the immense congregations of the following revival years. We were also rejoicing in the till then unexperienced help of an educated school master, a bright, fine looking man named Hooliamanu, who had lately graduated from Lahainaluna, and brought with him an atmosphere of incipient civilization. Some of our common people had advanced so far in apparel as to wear a shirt even on week-days. The head man and the schoolmaster could generally be found in pantaloons. The women were getting to wear at meetings the *holoku*, either of tapa or coarse cotton, generally the *pa-u* well wrapped over it. They had developed an immense form of straw bonnet, to which late styles show a tendency to revert. This was laden with exorbitant bows of tapa ribbon, usually dyed with gorgeous dabs of turmeric yellow and *noni* pink. The native ladies' tendency to amplitude in raiment about this time found special gratification in the new fashion of leg-of-mutton sleeves, introduced perhaps by our new reinforcement. These they expanded in tapa to balloon dimensions. The sight of entirely naked children previously so familiar at Kailua, was at Ewa more rare. Horses had hardly begun to be possessed by any natives. My father brought the first horned-cattle into the Ewa district. Goats were numerous. I had seldom tasted Irish potatoes or beef, and mutton never. We obtained a good supply of taro, poi, sweet potatoes, bananas, fish, pigs, fowls, and some very eatable native oysters and clams. Mr. Chamberlain supplied us with one barrel per annum of wormy flour, some very weevly rice, and some dark West India sugar and molasses, none then being made here. We had never heard of lucifer matches, and depended on the tinder box with flint and steel, using tin lamps with whale oil. The natives used chiefly the kukui candles or torches. It was very "plain living," but there was plenty of "high thinking."

Very prominent in the conditions of those times, was the overshadowing power of the haughty and arbitrary, yet kindly and beneficent chiefs, of whom Kekuanaoa and Kinau were those we most frequently saw at Ewa. The people were still serfs, accustomed to severe and irregular exactions of all sorts, and abjectly afraid of their lords. Kekuanaoa probably executed substantial justice and with much shrewdness. He was very determined and little disposed to be guided in secular matters by his religious teachers. I was on one occasion much impressed by my father's pain and indignation when he had failed to obtain the release of a party of Roman Catholic prisoners from Waianae, whom Kekuanaoa obdurately insisted on sentencing to hard labor for the crime of idolatry. This had been forbidden by Kaahumanu long before the French priests landed, and Kekuanaoa sternly refused to make any exception in their favor to the penalty for worshiping images, notwithstanding the earnest representations of Mr. Bingham and others.

In the missionary circle the General Meeting was the great center of social and spiritual interest. As the numbers and work of the missionaries increased, the sessions became more protracted, extending even to six weeks. Many of the older families took grass cottages and kept house in a sort of picnic way. How plainly I seem to see those temporary homes of the Thurstons, the Richards, the Gulicks, the Armstrongs and others. At the same time all the spare rooms and little out-rooms of the Binghams, Chamberlains, Judds, Tinkers, Dimonds, Halls, were overflowing with guests. Mrs. Chamberlain always kept open house for everybody.

The children were growing in size and number, Thurstons, Binghams, Richards, Judds, Andrews, Bishops, Gulicks, Greens, Clarks, Chamberlains, each contributed two or more old enough to unite under some lady teacher in daily classes during the meetings. Very delightful children's meetings were conducted first by Mr. Spaulding, and after his arrival by Mr. Coan, whom we children nearly worshipped, and to whose words many of us owed our first definite earnest drawings toward the Lord.

But the new school house at Kawaiahao was the chief center of interest, even to the older children among us. In the daily sessions of that now antiquated place there reigned an indescribably rich, fraternal, enthusiastic atmosphere of social and spiritual intercourse which is one of the most sacred and powerful things in all my memories of the past. It all rises before me somewhat as the Jerusalem experiences of a Christian child of the days after Pentecost might seem in the thoughts of his later life. There was a yearly deepening enthusiasm in the great Gospel work. There was a constantly strengthening confidence and more and more triumphant hope of the soon coming fulness of conquest of Hawaii for Christ. There was the earnest recounting in the station reports of labors and their fruits, the enthusiastic planning of new work. Their hearts kindled as they counselled and wrought together, and we children would easily kindle with our parents. We felt as if we, too, were sharers in the grand war and progressive triumph. All was going forward, hopeful, progressive. The Lord seemed visibly with his servants. Causes of difference and possible contention easily became merged in the onward movement. Some of our men and women were very ardent and joyful in their consecration, still kindled with the revival fire of Nettleton and Finney.

It was at this happy, eager and hopeful juncture of the Mission that the eagerly awaited Mary Frazier arrived with her thirty-two new helpers. I remember well our excitement and delight. The General Meeting was at hand, and soon met and absorbed this large new element. A majority of the men were lay teachers, giving a social variety in training and experience. We children saw a good deal of several of them. The youthful Bailey taught us in singing with great success. Mrs. Cooke trained our fingers in drawing. Marcia Smith kept school with the little ones. From this time on the new brothers and sisters constituted a very large element in the social and religious life of these Islands.

Their coming was timely. They held up the hands and cheered the spirits of the veteran workers. That very year the spiritual rains descended upon the whole nation and there was a mighty Pentecostal work. I think it was prior to the next General Meeting that I witnessed the admission of four hundred new members to my father's church in one day, in the presence of a congregation of six thousand people. Their baptism occupied two or three hours. It was administered to them in groups of ten or twelve, whose names were repeated in succession as the water was applied, followed by the baptismal formula for the whole group together.

The new teachers were of indispensable service in the new educational necessities. It is largely due to their aid that the Hawaiian people gained knowledge enough for the exercise of their new political privileges, so near at hand. Some of these brethren were ardently anti-slavery, and rather impatient of their old-fashioned elders. Rev. Dr. Lafon, a man of great ability, was especially active in setting the old missionaries right on that subject. They all kept native help or *ohuas* without regular wages, for their keep with food and clothing, and the position was counted as one of great advantage, as it was. Many of the old household servants rose to high station and property, by means of the superior intelligence so acquired. Dr. Lafon, however, denounced the relation as a species of slavery, and actually succeeded in making most, if not all, of the missionaries pay wages to their servants. I became more particularly acquainted with Mr. and Mrs. Locke, our neighbors at Waialua, and with the Van Duzees, who were for some months at Ewa. We saw much too of many others, and from the first their efficient help and fresh thoughts and ways were a continual comfort to their elder brethren. They were still "new missionaries" when I left the Islands, thirty months later. After a half a century of good service, a very few of these dear friends are enabled to rejoice with us in their Jubilee. I deeply rejoice to be permitted to sympathize with them, and help to recall those old days of their youth and early strength.

―――――o―――――

REMINISCENCES OF MISSIONARY LIFE.

BY J. W. SMITH. M. D.

On the morning of Sept. 21, 1842, the brig Sarah Abigail, after a voyage of 142 days from Boston, dropped anchor off the port of Honolulu. Soon after a boat came from the shore bringing two young chiefs, Prince Lot and Prince Alexander, and my brother-in-law, Mr. H. O. Knapp, one of the reinforcement of 1837, whose Jubilee we now celebrate. About 11 A. M., we landed and met Mr. Chamberlain on the wharf who conducted us to the old Bingham house, where the missionaries had assembled to welcome the new comers. I remember that most of them looked pale, and careworn, but they all gave us a very hearty welcome. In the afternoon of the same day Rev.

Mr. Armstrong took me up to Punahou. The plain was very dry and dusty; very little vegetation was to be seen, and hardly a tree or house in sight. I thought of the deserts of Africa. Today, as I rode across the same plain I could but wonder at the great change. The forest of algeroba and other trees, the numerous and beautiful cottages, with here and there a fine mansion, combine to make a wonderful contrast. The Rev. D. Dole, Mrs. Dole and Miss Marcia Smith were then the teachers at Punahou.

My first professional work at the islands was to visit Mrs. Locke, at Waialua. She had been sick several weeks, and I found her very low; but she recognized her brother, Rev. G. B. Rowell, who was with me. Mrs. Locke lingered a few days and then passed over the river to the shining shore, leaving a husband and three little children to mourn her loss. Mr. and Mrs. Locke were also passengers by the Mary Frazier.

Early in November, we left Honolulu for Kauai in Ladd & Co.'s little schooner, the Hawaii, Capt. Spunyarn. At the landing at Koloa we found a good company of natives waiting, who gave us their warm aloha. There was a comfortable house at Koloa ready for us. It was built by Dr. Lafon who had left the mission. Two days after our arrival at Koloa, Father Whitney, from Waimea, came to see us, bringing a Hingham bucket, full of nice things for the table, sent by Mrs. Whitney, who supposed such things would be acceptable to us strangers among the natives of whose language we then knew but few words. My recollections of Father Whitney are very pleasant. He was of rather large stature, of pleasant manners, very companionable and generous almost to a fault. He was one of nature's noblemen, and a model missionary. No man ever lived on Kauai more beloved and respected than Rev. Samuel Whitney. There were several foreign residents at Koloa on our arrival there, who received us kindly and did us many favors. I must not omit in such a paper as this, the names of Mr. and Mrs. Burnham and Mr. and Mrs. Goodale. They were true Christian friends, and did us many acts of kindness, but they soon left the islands and went back to the States. Mr. Burnham is still living in Philadelphia; and Mrs. Goodale has recently returned to Honolulu to spend the remnant of her days with her daugter, Mrs. Wolfe. Father Peter J. Gulick ought also to be mentioned in this connection. He established the missionary station at Koloa in 1834, and labored there for about eight years, and many were added to the Church under his ministration. Nearly 45 years have passed by. All my missionary brethren on the island of Kauai have rested from their labors, and a whole generation of Hawaiians have passed away.

In 1861, we established a boarding school for native and half caste girls at Koloa. Mrs. Smith and her sister, Miss Deborah Knapp, and our daughters were the teachers. We continued the school for ten years. Some of the girls on leaving the school turned out badly for a while; but many of them have since done well. I will mention the case of one of them: She was nine years old when she entered the school, a bright, lively girl a little disposed to be mischievous. She made good progress, however, in her studies, and soon got hold of the English language so as to speak it very well. She did not stay to complete the course of study. Her father came to see her, and was so pleased with her improvement that he must take her home at once. It would be so nice to have such a civilized and intelligent girl in his house. Our remonstrances were of no avail, and he took her from the school. The girl's mother was dead, and she had no good and wise friend to watch over her; and her course was just what we might expect of a native girl left in such circumstances. We heard only evil reports of her for a year or two, and then we lost sight of her entirely. For a dozen years we heard nothing definite from this girl. It is but recently that Miss Mary Green, in her visitation at Kapalama, found her, a woman now, 34 or 35 years old. She is married, and living with her husband in their own house. She has been engaged in teaching for several years— has a private school of over fifty children; is a member of the church at that place, has a class in the Sabbath school, and has a good reputation. I visited her last week, and it was affecting to hear her express her gratitude for the instructions she received in the Koloa Boarding School. She also expressed deep regret for the years she had wasted in sinful ways; and she attributed her present blessings to God's answer to the prayers of her teachers. I mention the case of this girl for the encouragement of those engaged in teaching Hawaiian girls.

As reminiscences are the subject before us, it may be allowable for me to relate some of the special providences which Mrs. Smith and I have experienced in our missionary life. And first, I would mention our voyage from Boston to the Islands. The ship Victoria was to sail from New York about March 1, 1842. Among the passengers were Mother Thurston and her children returning to the Islands. Rev. S. C. Damon, Seamen's Chaplin for the port of Honolulu, and Mrs. Damon were also on board. They would be good company, we thought, for the long voyage. We were ready, but the Secretaries at Boston would not send us. I asked one of them why they did not send us then, and his only answer was, "It is all right." Well, just fifty days after the sailing of lhe Victoria, we embarked at Boston on board the afore-mentioned brig, Sarah Abigail, a small vessel with poor accommodations for so long a voyage. Neither the captain or any of his officers had ever been round Cape Horn, and we were to pass the dreaded cape in mid-winter. Some of our friends were anxious about us. And, yet, notwithstanding the bad prospect, we had a favorable voyage to Honolulu, and arrived there four weeks before the Victoria. We remembered the saying of the Secretary, that "it was all right."

Another circumstance I will mention, was on being located on Kauai. I was sent to the Islands as a missionary physician, and was told in Boston that I would probably be stationed at Kailua, on the Island of Hawaii, to take the place of Dr. Andrews, who was wanted at Lahainaluna. And it was a surprise to us on arriving at Honolulu to hear that we had been already assigned to the station at Koloa, Kauai, to take the place left vacant by Dr. Lafon, who had left the mission. Well, this, too, "was all right." Koloa is a place greatly in contrast with Kailua; and, considering the state of my health, it was far better for me to travel around "the garden island," rather than among the clinkers of Hawaii. We have always been thankful that our lot was cast at Koloa instead of Kailua.

I will mention but one other instance of the kind providence which has accompanied us through all our missionary life. In April, 1853, we had made arrangements to attend the General Meeting at Honolulu. We embarked on board the schooner Chance. Her cabin was very small. We spread mats on the floor and bunked down with our little children. With a strong head wind and rough sea, how we spent that night they can imagine who remember schooner voyaging of thirty years ago. The next day we discovered that there was no fire wood on board the schooner, and that no cooking could be done till we reached Honolulu. When twenty-four hours out we had sailed about twelve miles, and were close to the shore off Nawiliwili. The prospect was discouraging, and I persuaded the captain to put us on shore, and we gave up the idea of going to the General Meeting that year. Now, all this was not an extraordinary experience for those days of schooner voyaging; but here is the sequel. Two days after landing at Nawiliwili, we heard the small pox was raging at Honolulu, and the natives were dying at a fearful rate. Certainly it was a kind overruling providence that prevented us going into the infected city. And, moreover, the disease was sure to visit Kauai sooner or later, and it was clearly my duty, as the only physician on the island, to remain here. A few days later I received a supply of vaccine virus and began to vaccinate the entire population of Kauai.

"Man's heart deviseth his way,
But the Lord directeth his steps."

———o———

A GENERAL REVIEW OF THE MISSION WORK IN HAWAII.

BY HON. S. N. CASTLE.

This mission was organized in the State of Massachusetts in the autumn of 1819, and embarked from the city of Boston for the islands the same year upon the brig Thaddeus, arriving here in March, 1820. The pioneers consisted of four clergymen, one printer, one physician and one farmer. They were all married, and the farmer had three sons and two daughters—14 adults and 5 children. Cook, in 1778, had found the people in a heathen and savage state. From that time, but more especially from Vancouver's visit in 1792, foreign intercourse and trade had been increasing. The chiefs had learned to value sandal wood, and derived from it quite a revenue. They had become familiar with white faces and perhaps passed from the savage to the barbarous state. Their garb, or rather that of the chiefs, had improved, but little had been done to improve their morals. Through most of these years, the great Hawaiian chief, Kamehameha I, had been carrying forward his conquest of the islands until he had brought them all under his sway. On the 8th of May, 1819, about forty years after the first visit of Cook, and about twenty-seven years after Vancouver's visit of 1792, Kamehameha died.

"Vancouver wisely refused to purchase supplies with arms and ammunition, and it was then that attention was first turned towards sandal wood, as an article of export." The income derived from this source was one year $400,000. Vessels and cargoes were bought at exorbitant prices. Heavy debts were created. Luxury and dissipation were engendered. The people were oppressed for a score of years in gathering the precious wood, and otherwise, to relieve the King and chiefs of the debts sorely pressing upon them, the fruits of their extravagance. But such was the condition of chiefs and people when the missionaries first landed here, in March, 1820, sixty-seven years ago. Ignorant, shameless, in dress and manners, such that Christianized and civilized men and women felt that women of like sensibilities could not live there. Said the owner of one of the trading vessels of this group and ocean, who saw them embarking, "Those women are fools. They cannot live there, and will, every one of them, be back within a year, and I have given my captains orders to give them their passages whenever they apply." They never applied. The speaker did not appreciate their qualities of Christian heroism. True, some of these and others, years after, when worn down with labors for their Hawaiian sisters, that *they* might be enlightened and saved, and in training their own families, as well, have found rest in their native land, and some have found it on the shining shore, where there is rest for the weary; but none have abandoned their work because its repugnance tried their souls. The missionaries came to Christianize and civilize, and for that purpose used the means adapted to that end. Heathenism must give way to Christianity, barbarism to civilization, ignorance to letters, and despotism to righteous rule. The first step was the acquisition of the language and its reduction to writing, and the first experiment in printing was made on the 7th of January, 1822—about 22 months from their first landing. On the 11th of August, 1822, the first Christian marriage was performed. In February, 1823, a law was proclaimed for the observance of the Sabbath. In March, 1823, Hoapili and Keopuolani, high chiefs, were married. Gradually the chiefs and people yielded to the instructions of the missionaries, and schools and churches were established. I connot here enter into the history of the blessing that followed the labors of the missionaries until the great revival of 1837-9, nor the history of the evil that was wrought through the influence of one man. Truly, "one sinner destroyeth much good." Early in the thirties, Kamehameha III, then a minor, had a retainer named *Kaomi* attached to his person— a sprightly, shrewd young man. He was early instructed, made good progress, and became a teacher, and after four or five years desired baptism, but it was not granted. He changed his course and plunged into dissipation, and acquired a great and pernicious influence over the Prince and others, and led them into evil courses. The land was filled with drinking and dissipation, and the missionaries' hearts with anxiety; but whilst the Prince was going astray and exerting a baneful influence, the old chiefs adhered with great steadfastness to the Christianity which they had chosen, and when the Prince arrived at his majority, and the reins of government passed into his hands, greatly to the joy of the missionaries he chose his counsellors from the Christian chiefs instead of his boon companions.

The great success which had crowned the missionary labors from the first, had opened an ever-widening door and called for constant reinforcements, the necessity, for which, was continually emphasized, as the years rolled on, by one laborer after another, dropping in their footsteps worn with disease and labor, and others in their feebleness, seeking a restoration of health and strength went home to die. The American Board of Missions ever ready to respond to the calls of its missionaries, according to the measure of its ability, had, prior to 1837, within the first seventeen years of the establishment of the Mission, sent to their aid six reinforcements, consisting of 34 men and their wives, and two unmarried women, making, including the pioneers, 41 married couples and 2 single ladies, 84 in all. Of these, 21 had returned and 5 died=26, leaving on the ground 58 missionaries, 2 of them being single ladies. The 7th and largest reinforcement sent out by the A. B. C. F. M., numbered 15 married couples and 2 single ladies, 32 in all. There were four clergymen, one of whom was a physician; one physician in addition; nine teachers and one secular agent, with wives, and two single ladies. For the passage of this company to the Islands, the treasurer of the Board chartered the bark Mary Frazier, of 288 tons burthen, but of double that carrying capacity. She sailed from Boston December 14, 1836; doubled Cape Horn the 12th of February, 1837, and anchored off Honolulu 2 P. M., Sunday, April 9, 1837, after the short passage of 116 days. She landed her passengers at 10 A. M. the next day, and they were cordially received by the missionaries of the station; also by the King and chiefs, of whom about twenty in number were present on the occasion.

Noteworthy incidents of the voyage and reception and the particular locations of work of this company will probably be given by others who were members of it. The common relations which I have borne to the whole Mission has led me to a more general review of its work, although it is the semi-centennial of the arrival of the *seventh* reinforcement that we are gathered to celebrate. Prior to the advent of this reinforcement, 1,259 had been admitted to the Church, 1,049 of whom remained in good standing. This was on the eve of the great revival in which large numbers were admitted to the Church. In 1840, I find 18,451 remaining in regular standing. Schools and the press had done much towards establishing the foundations of a Christian civilization. Progress, too, had been made in political enfranchisement. The first constitution was granted by the King in 1840, and with the code of laws, issued, eighteen years after the language was reduced to writing, and the first experiment made in printing. Schools were prosperous, and a large part of the Hawaiians could read. The Bible had been translated and other books of a healthful character been written, and translated and compiled, and widely circulated.

The rulers and the people were generally on the side of good order, and they were teachable. The future prospect was hopeful as far as their religions and civil life was concerned, and the shadows which rested upon their future, as a people, were lightened by the hopes stimulated by their favorable moral and religious condition. Since the visit of Cook, they had been steadily diminishing. Vancouver, who was with Cook in his visits to the Islands, was saddened, in his visit a few years later by the great apparent diminution of the population. Cook, in 1778, *estimated* them at 400,000. In 1823, 45 years later, they were *estimated* at 142,050; nine years later, in 1832, the *census* gave 130,313; four years later still, in 1836, the *census* gave 108,579.

This rapid decadence was discouraging to the hopes of national perpetuity, but it was supposed to be due in a great measure to the wars of conquest, pestilence, disease, hardships and exposure, and other causes, which would be modified or removed by the adoption of Christian principles and practise. Our hopes in this direction, lay in the reform of adults and training of the children aright. I need not say that our expectations have not been fully realized.

The census of 1850 gave 87,202, a decrease in 14 years of..................................23,414
The census of 1860 gave 67,064, a decrease in 10 years of..................................15,139
The census of 1866 gave 58,765, a decrease in 6 years of................................... 8,299
The census of 1884 gave 44,232, a decrease in 14 years of..................................14,533

                                                                                         62,385

These figures include pure Hawaiians and half-castes. The total decrease in the half century has been 62,385; and from the census of 1832 to that of 1884, a period of 52 years, a diminution of 86,08I, being a steady decrease, contrary to all our hopes.

Mr. Jarves says, "A missionary upon inquiring of a Bible class of 80 married women, how many had been mothers, found but 39. Nine of the mission families numbered 59 children. Twenty Hawaiian chiefs have but 19 children among them all." By recent investigation it has been ascertained that to 67 mission families there were

359 children, of whom 95 have died, leaving 264 living, or 4 to each family out of an average of 5 4-10 born to each family; and out of the 67 families there remains about 25 families, or 51 persons, making of parents and children living, 300, or an increase of population in the first generation of 240 per cent., whilst the whole number of descendants of the 65 families counts more than 800 individuals now living. It is these discouraging facts which disheartens the friends of Hawaii as to the perpetuity of the race and its institutions, but they nevertheless feel constrained to do all in their power for their spiritual and temporal welfare, being fully persuaded they can only be saved through Bible principles and practise. In harmony with this subject and of some interest as an episode embraced within the period of this semi-centennial, I have thought this Society might be interested in a brief account of the presentation of a Bible from the American Bible Society to His Majesty Kamehameho IV, on the 26th day of May, 1857.

Some of my auditors were perhaps present on that occasion. If so, I hope to be so brief as not to weary them, whilst I trust it may be of some interest to those who were not there. I will read the remarks made on that occasion, with the interesting and appropriate response made by His Majesty. They are as follows:

"I must beg the indulgence of Your Majesty in listening to the few brief remarks which I have to offer on this occasion. I not only desire that they may be acceptable to Your Majesty, but meet the approbation of the King of Kings, before whom kings and subjects stand on one common level, and at whose august Tribunal they must alike give up their account.

MAY IT PLEASE YOUR MAJESTY:—By the request of the Secretary of the American Bible Society, I have the honor and the pleasure of presenting to Your Majesty a copy of the Holy Scriptures, the gift of that noble institution, together with a letter in its behalf from its revered and honored Secretary.

This Society is not altogether unknown to Your Majesty. It is an honored member of the great family of benevolent societies, whose object is to give the Gospel to the whole race of man. The *special* mission of *this* institution, in co-operation with other kindred societies, is to carry the Word of God to every nation and people in its own tongue, that all may be partakers of its blessings.

The British and Foreign Bible Society may be said to stand at the head of this noble class of institutions. Since its formation, the Scriptures have been translated into one hundred and forty-eight languages and dialects, one hundred and twenty-one of which were previously unknown, and twenty-five had existed without an alphabet; and more than forty-three millions of copies have been circulated amongst not less than six hundred millions of peoyle.

The errand of these Societies is one of peace and good will to men. Bound, indeed, to universal conquest, the triumph of the Bible is not that of arms. Unlike the progress of earthly conquerors, its onward march is heralded by no confused noise of trampling and prancing of horses, no roar of artillery, no clangor of arms, no groans of the wounded and dying, no garments of warriors rolled in blood, but it comes noiselessy, winning its way to the heart. Its triumph is the triumph of love.

The Bible is the harbinger of civil and social blessings. Its teachings, received and obeyed, bring joy and gladness into the family, the community, the body politic. It makes good husbands and wives, parents and children, brothers and sisters, neighbors and friends, kings and subjects. It is adapted to all classes—the high and low, the rich and poor, the learned and unlearned, the king on his throne and the peasant in his cottage. It comes with blessings to all. Darkness, before it, brightens into day. Civil and religious despotism flee its approach, for it bears upon its pages the rich treasures of civil and religious liberty. It teaches that rulers must be just, ruling in the fear of God; and the reciprocal duty of obedience to righteous and just laws, upon the part of the ruled. Of its power to bless and renovate, Your Majesty has occular demonstration in the condition of your own people. Scarcely has a generation passed away since the first glimmering of its beams fell upon these isles shrouded in the long night of ages. What were they then? Barbarous, benighted, without any knowledge of the true God, without schools, or books, or churches, with a despotic government and priesthood, with whose bloody rites mingled, at times, the cries of human victims with gods upon whose altars flowed their blood. What are they now? Barbarism and darkness have fled away. The true God is known and worshipped, schools, and books, and churches, fill the land. Upon their altars smoke no bloody sacrifices, but from them ascends the grateful incense of prayer and praise to Him who has not proclaimed peace and good will to men. A Constitutional Government and just laws have arisen for the mutual benefit of King and people. How great the change! In vain shall we scan the pages of history to find its parallel, in the brief period of time which has elapsed during its progress.

What has produced this change? I answer, the Bible. Yes, the Bible given to this people by the American Bible Society, and I digress to say that we have with us, to-day, one of the honored surviving patriarchs who has seen it all; yea, more, has aided through it all; nor would I forget those female helpers, who, thirty-eight years ago, in the vigor of youth, embarked in an untried, and what was then by many regarded as a hopeless enterprise, who forsook the endearments of home and civilization, and with a moral courage not inferior to that physical courage displayed on the fields of Inkerman and Balaclava, dared the dangers of a vast ocean, which no civilized female had traversed before, that they might do good to their race. Venerable men and women, we will rejoice with you in the reward you are receiving to-day. Pardon this digression, for it seemed in harmony with the subject to refer to those who had been largely instrumental in producing this change.

But, whilst such are the blessings which flow from this Bible, it also says that sin is a reproach to any people, and the nation and kingdom that will not serve the Lord shall perish. It has temporal blessings and temporal judgments. It has likewise those which belong to the world to come. It brings life and immortality to light. It reveals the only Savior who can deliver from the wrath to come. It opens up the only pathway of our fallen race to the rest of the heavenly Jerusalem. To those who embrace and obey it, its blessings are unspeakable. To those who reject it, its denunciations are fearful.

Such, Sire, is the book which. in the name and in behalf of the American Bible Society, I have the honor of presenting to Your Majesty to-day; and permit me to add the assurance of the earnest prayers of the donors, as well as of every Christian heart, that it may be received as your guide; that practising its precepts in the administration of your government as well as private life, you may escape its denunciations and participate in its blessings, both in this life and that which is to come."

HIS MASESTY'S REPLY.

"The volume you present me in behalf of the American Bible Society, and the letter with which it is accompanied, I receive with a mingled feeling of pleasure and reverence. When I remember the moral illumination and the sense of social propriety which have spread throughout these islands, in proportion as the Holy Scriptures have been circulated, I cannot but admire and respect the human agency through which Providence has effected its benign purpose. But of all the members of the institution, there is none with whom I could more gladly find myself in communication than the Secretary, whose labors have won for him a name among Christian philanthropists which might excite a world to emulation.

I will not attempt to echo the tone of fervent admiration and gratitude with which you allude to the happy changes effected by the dissemination of God's Holy Word. But from the position I occupy, the facts meet me whichever way I turn my eyes. I see them every day and every hour. I see principles taking root among my people that were unknown, and unintelligible to them at that dark period of our religious history to which you have referred. They have now a standard by which to judge of themselves and of each other as members of society. Without that standard no law but the law of autocratic power could have ruled them. Its absence would have rendered the gift of free institutions, such as they now enjoy, a worse than useless act of magnanimity on the part of my predecessors. The commerce and intercourse with other countries to which we owe our present prosperity would have been checked by numberless difficulties. In one word we see through all onr relations the effect of those aspirations and principles inculcated by this sacred volume.

I should be wanting to myself did I not express the gratification I feel in seeing here present some of those who were first to labor in the vineyard. Although they look for their reward elsewhere, they will not reject my passing tribute of respect. Their labor has been long and their anxiety great, but their constancy and patience have equaled the emergency. The result of their life's work may even disappoint them if they judge it by the anticipation of their more sanguine years. Yet, in their decline of life, they see some of the fruits they prayed for, and they will not complain, when they remember that the measure of their success is from above.

Allow me to thank you for your personal share in the presentation, and through you to express my kindest acknowledgements to the American Bible Society."

It is a cause for rejoicing, that the blessing of God upon Christian instruction, had made it possible for the King truthfully to make such a response. When it is remembered that both his father and his mother were born in a savage state, in the darkness of heathenism, a score of years before a ray of the blessed light of the Gospel ever beamed upon them, that the whole of their youth was under such adverse influences the change seems marvellous. Well might the King say of these changes in this land, "I see them every day and every hour and whichever way I turn my eyes." After they embraced Christianity, their influence and that of thousands of others was steadfastly in its favor nntil their course was finished. Whilst the missionaries sorrow, that no more has been accomplished, that they cannot now look upon the race and nation as the repositories of a vigorous Christian and physical life, they rejoice that so much has been done. Of the Seventh Reinforcement, the semi-centennial of whose arrival we now celebrate, numbering thirty-two, eleven only remain; twenty-one have passed away. Only one of the fifteen married couple remains unbroken. The now venerable and honored Father and Mother Bailey, the youngest of the band, still live, and this fiftieth year of their labors closes the seventy-third of their lives. May they long be spared. Of the one hundred and sixty who have embarked in this work, one hundred and sixteen have finished their course, forty-four remain, most of whom are laden with the infirmities of age and will soon join their fellow-laborers who have preceded them. The work which *they, your* fathers and mothers, begun is not finished. Children of missionaries, members of the Cousins' Society, Christians who sympathize with them in the work to be done for the Savior, this work is yours. It is a great work but you have an almighty helper, and if you enter upon it, in reliance upon Him you will not be confounded. Whether the decadence of the Hawaiian race goes on or not, it is certain that it can be arrested *in no other way*, than by heeding the instructions of the Bible, by the practise of temperance and the virtues which it inculcates. In this is their only hope of salvation, and if national decay is not arrested, as our prayer has been that it might, be, yet as we have seen large numbers of *individuals* in the past forsake the wrong and embrace the right. So *you* may labor with hopes of the same blessing upon *your* labors in time to come. you may see many saved, though national decadence may continue to go on, to entire extinction. It is yours to labor and pray. It is God's to answer and bless. He has done so in the salvation of thousands of Hawaiians in the past, whilst national decay has still gone on. It may be so in time to come. Individuals may be saved. The nation may perish or be swallowed up in others.

In closing, I beg to say a few words of the "Mission Children's Society," whose guests we have the honor of being to-day.

On the 5th day of June, 1852, a generation ago, one of their number being on his way to aid in planting a Micronesian Islands mission, a goodly number of missionary children, of all ages, gathered in the school house to organize a society to actively aid in the good work of their parents, in this, and other lands as the door might open, and the call might come.

A generation has passed, young people have become parents, and grand parents. The Society has increased from few in number to hundreds. Scattered through the world, the aggregae income, since its formation to $20,000. The good done in the field, beyond estimation. Some have taken up the work begun by their parents here, some bear aloft the banner of the cross in other lands shrouded in darkness, others are living useful lives in almost every honorable department of human activity. Upon the bench and at the bar. In the healing profession and work of education; and in the paths of agriculture and commerce, and in different and distant parts of the world. Some from the the outside, of like hopes and inspirations have joined this Society, and labor in harmony to save others not so highly favored, but the great body of its members are descendants of those who left home and country to save the Hawaiian and win him to Christ. Never, perhaps, had so large a society such a unique parentage. About three-fourths of the whole of the men were ordained ministers of the Gospel. Others were professional men, and of avocations calling for intelligence and mental discipline, and withal highly conscientious. They, too, men and women, were the children of the pilgrims, men and women. Nature's nobility, who, in the dawn of religious freedom, had dared the perils and hardships of the wilderness and the cruelty of the savage that they might worship God according to the dictates of their own consciences. Well were they fitted to be the founders of the free Anglo-

American empire, the great self-governing empire of the world. Men who chose to derive their nobility from their manhood rather than any less worthy source. Such, near and remote is the ancestry of this Society, and the work it is called to aid in doing, is more worthy of its ancestry. It is to win souls to Christ, not fainting by the way, until the kingdoms of the world shall become "the kingdoms of the Lord and of His Christ."

———o———

CATALOGUE, ALPHABETICALLY ARRANGED, OF THE
THE A. B C F: M. OF BOSTON, AND THE

Number of Reinforce.	NAMES OF MISSIONARIES.	PLACE OF BIRTH.
4	Alexander, Rev. Wm. P	Paris, Ky
4	Alexander, Mrs. Mary A.(McKinney)	Wilmington, Del..
10	Andrews, Rev. C. B	Kinsman, O
10	Addrews, Mrs. Ann S. (Gilson)	Reading. Vt
	Andrews, Mrs. Samantha (Gilson)	Reading, Vt
7	Andrews, Dr. Seth L	Putney, Vt
7	Andrews, Mrs. Parnelly (Pierce)	Woodbury, Conn..
	Andrews, Mrs. Amelia T. (Dike)	Pittsford, Vt
4	Armstrong, Rev. Richard, D. D	Turbottville, Pa
4	Amstrong, Mrs. Clarissa (Chapman)	Russell, Mass
2	Andrews, Rev. Lorrin	East Windsor,Conn
2	Andrews, Mrs. Mary A. (Wilson)	Mayville, Ky
7	Bailey, Edward	Holden, Mass
7	Bailey, Mrs. Caroline (Hubbard)	Holden, Mass
3	Baldwin, Rev. Dwight, M. D	Durham, Conn
3	Baldwin, Mrs. Charlotte (Fowler)	Northford, Conn...
14	Baldwin, Rev. Wm. O	Greenfield, N. H
14	Baldwin, Mrs. Mary (Proctor)	Lunenburg, Mass..
P	Bingham, Rev. Hiram	Bennington, Vt
P	Bingham, Mrs. Sybil (Moseley)	Westfield, Mass
	Bingham, Mrs. N. E. (Morse)	Westfield, Mass
1	Blatchley, Dr. Abraham	East Guilford, Conn
1	Blatchley, Mrs. Jemima (Marvin)	Lyme, Conn
7	Bliss, Rev. Isaac	Warren, Mass
7	Bliss, Mrs. Emily (Curtis)	Elbridge, N. Y
1	Bishop, Rev. Artemus	Pompey, N. Y
1	Bishop, Mrs. Elizabeth (Edwards)	Marlboro, Mass
2	Bishop, Mrs. Delia (Stone)	Bloomfield, N. Y..
8	Bond, Rev. Elias	Hallowell, Me
8	Bond, Mrs. Ella M. (Howell)	Portland, Me
6	Brown, Miss Lydia	Wilton, N. H
7	Castle, Sam'l N	Cazenovia, N. Y
7	Castle, Mrs. Angeline (Tenney)	Sudbury, Vt
	Castle, Mrs. Mary A. (Tenney)	Plainfield, N. Y
P	Chamberlain, Daniel	Brookfield, Mass
P	Chamberlain, Mrs. Jerusha	Brookfield, Mass

129

MISSIONARIES AT THE HAWAIIAN ISLANDS SENT BY SEAMENS' FRIEND SOCIETY OF N. Y.

Year of Birth.	Year of Arrival.	Date of Return.	Date of Death.	Number of Children.	Number of Grand Ch'n	Great Gr'nd Children.	Total Descendants.	Desc'nd'nts Living.
1805	1832		1884	9	33		42	39
1810	1832							
1817	1844		1879	6	7		13	10
1823	1852		1862					
1828	1863	1879						
1809	1837	1849		4	3		7	2
1807	1837		1846					
1815								
1805	1832		1860	10	18	2	30	20
1805	1837	1880						
1796	1828		1868	7	22	2	31	26
1804	1828		1879					
1814	1837			5	13	6	24	20
1814	1837							
1798	1831		1886	8	25		33	30
1805	1831		1873					
1821	1855	1860		3			3	2
1821	1855	1860						
1789	1820	1840	1869	7	19	9	35	24
1798	1820	1840	1848					
1804			1873					
	1823	1826	1860					
1791	1823	1826	*					
1804	1837	1841	1851	1	3		4	2
1811	1837	1841	1866					
1795	1823		1872	2	7	1	10	7
1798	1823		1828					
1800	1828		1875					
1813	1841			10	11		21	18
1817	1841		1881					
1780	1835		1869					
1808	1837			11	18		29	22
1810	1837		1841					
1819	1843							
	1820	1823	1881	5			5	5
	1820	1823	1879					

* Probably dead.

11*

CATALOGUE, ALPHABETICALLY ARRANGED, OF THE
THE A. B. C. F. M. OF BOSTON, AND THE

Number of Reinforc.	NAMES OF MISSIONARIES.	PLACE OF BIRTH.
1	Chamberlain, Levi	Dover, Vt.
2	Chamberlain, Mrs. Maria (Patten)	Salisbury, Pa.
4	Chapin, Alonzo, M. D	W. Springf'ld, Mass
4	Chapin, Mrs. Mary A. (Tenney)	Newburyport, Mass
2	Clark, Rev. Ephraim W	Haverhill, N. H.
2	Clark, Mrs. Mary (Kittredge)	Mt. Vernon, N. H..
	Clark, Mrs. Sarah H. (Richards)	Norwich, Vt.
6	Coan, Rev. Titus	Killingworth, Conn
6	Coan, Mrs. Fidelia (Church)	Riga, N. Y.
	*Coan, Mrs. Lydia (Bingham)	Honolulu, H. I.
7	Conde, Rev. Daniel T.	Charlton, N. Y.
7	Conde, Mrs. Andelusia (Lee)	Jericho, Vt.
	Conde, Mrs. 2nd (name not known)	
7	Cooke, Amos Starr	Danbury, Conn.
7	Cooke, Mrs. Juliette (Montague)	Sunderland, Mass..
	Damon, Rev. Sam'l C., D. D	Holden, Mass.
	Damon, Mrs. Julia (Mills)	Torringford Conn..
3	Dibble, Rev. Sheldon	Skeneatles, N. Y.
3	Dibble, Mrs. Maria M. (Tomlinson)	Troy, N. Y.
	Dibble, Mrs. Antoinette (Tomlinson)	Manlius, N. Y.
	Diell, Rev. John	Cherry Valley, N.Y.
	Diell, Mrs. Caroline A	Plattsburg, N. Y.
6	Dimond, Henry	Fairfield, Conn.
6	Dimond, Mrs. Anna M. (Anner)	N. Y. City, N. Y.
8	Dole, Rev. Daniel	Bloomfield, Me.
8	Dole, Mrs. Emily H. Ballard	Hallowell, Me.
7	Dole, Mrs. *Charlotte C. Knapp*	
11	Dwight, Rev. Samuel G	Northh'mpt'n, Mass
	Dwight, Mrs Anna (Mahoe)	Molokai, H. I.
	Ellis, Rev. William	England
	Ellis, Mrs. Mary (Moor)	Londan, England..
	Ellis, Mrs. Sarah (Stickney)	England.
4	Emerson, Rev. John S	Chester, N. H.
4	Emerson, Mrs. Ursula S. (Newell)	Nelson, N. H.
1	Ely, Rev. James F	Lyme, Conn.
1	Ely, Mrs. Louisa S. (Everest)	Cornwall, Conn.

*Daughter of missionary.

MISSIONARIES AT THE HAWAIIAN ISLANDS SENT BY SEAMENS' FRIEND SOCIETY OF N. Y.

Year of Birth.	Year of Arrival.	Date of Return.	Date of Death.	Number of Children.	Number of Grand Ch'n	Great Gr'nd Children.	Total Descendants.	Desc'nd'nts Living.
1792	1823		1849	8	17		25	21
1803	1828		1880					
1805	1832	1835	1876	1			1	1
1804	1832	1835	1885					
1799	1828	1864	1878	8	28	1	37	29
1803	1828		1857					
	1859	1864						
1801	1835		1882	4	4		8	6
1810	1835		1872					
1834								
1807	1837	1855		7	9		16	14
1810	1837		1855					
1810	1837		1871	7	23		30	25
1812	1837							
1815	1842		1885	5	8		13	11
1817	1842							
1809	1831		1845	6	8	3	17	13
1808	1831		1837					
1809	1840	1845						
	1833		1841	4	14		18	14
1807	1833	1841						
1808	1835			7	20		27	17
1808	1835							
1808	1841		1878	2	11		13	13
1808	1841		1844					
1815	1848		1880	6	6		12	9
1839			1879					
	1823	1824	dead	4			4	4
1793	1823	1824	1835					
			dead					
1800	1832		1867	8	5		13	9
1806	1832							
1798	1823	1828	dead					
1792	1823	1828	dead					

CATALOGUE, ALPHABETICALLY ARRANGED, OF THE
THE A. B. C. F. M. OF BOSTON, AND THE

Number of Reinforce.	NAMES OF MISSIONARIES	PLACE OF BIRTH.
4	Forbes, Rev. Cochran................	Goshen, Pa.........
4	Forbes, Mrs. Rebecca D. (Smith)....	Springfield, N. J...
5	Fuller, Lemuel......................	Attleboro, Mass....
1	Goodrich, Rev. Joseph...............	Wethersfield, Conn.
1	Goodrich, Mrs. Martha (Barnes).....	Connecticut.......
2	Green, Rev. Jonathan S..............	Lebanon, Conn....
2	Green, Mrs. Theodosia S. (Arnold)...	E. Haddam, Conn..
	Green, Mrs. Asenath C. (Spring)....	Brimfield, Conn...
2	Gulick, Rev. Peter J.	Freehold, N. J.....
2	Gulick, Mrs. Fanny H. (Thomas)....	Lebanon, Conn....
6	Hall, Edwin O......................	Walpole, N. H.....
6	Hall, Mrs. Sarah L. (Williams)......	Elizabethtown,N.J.
	Hall, Mrs. Mary (Dame).............	Falmouth, Me.....
4	Hitchcock, Rev. Harvey R...........	Gt. Barrinton, Mass
4	Hitchcock, Mrs. Rebecca (Howard)..	Owasco, N. Y.....
P	Holman, Dr. Thomas................	Cooperstown, N. Y
P	Holman, Mrs. Lucia (Ruggles).......	Brooklyn, Conn. ..
10	Hunt, Rev. T. Dwight...............	Rochester, N. Y...
10	Hunt, Mrs. Mary (Hedges)	Newark, N. J......
	Hunt, Mrs. 2nd (name not known)...	
	Hunt, Mrs. 3d (name not known)....	
16	Hyde, Rev. Charles M...............	New York City....
16	Hyde, Mrs. Mary (Knight)...........	Brimfield, Mass....
7	Ives, Rev. Mark....................	Goshen, Conn.....
7	Ives, Mrs. Mary A. (Brainard).......	Haddam, Conn. ..
7	Johnson, Rev. Edward..............	Hollis, N. H.......
7	Johnson, Mrs Lois S. (Hoyt)........	Salisbury, N. H....
2	Judd, Dr. Gerrit P..................	Paris, N. Y........
2	Judd, Mrs Laura (Fish).............	Plainfield, N. Y....
3	Johnstone, Andrew.................	Dundee, Scotland..
3	Johnstone, Mrs. Rebecca (Worth)....	Nantucket, Mass...
11	Kinney, Rev. Henry....	Amenia, N. Y.....
11	Kinney, Mrs. Maria L. (Walsworth)..	Cleveland, O ......
7	Knapp, Horton O	Greenwich, Conn..
7	Knapp, Mrs. Charlotte (Close).......	Greenwich, Conn..
7	Lafon, Dr. Thomas.................	Chesterfield Co., Va

MISSIONARIES AT THE HAWAIIAN ISLANDS SENT BY SEAMENS' FRIEND SOCIETY OF N. Y.

Year of Birth.	Year of Arrival.	Date of Return.	Date of Death.	Number of Children.	Number of Grand Ch'n.	Great Gr'nd Children.	Total Descendants.	Desc'nd'nts Living.
1805	1832	1847	1880	5	9		14	8
1805	1832	1847	1878					
1810	1833	1834	*					
	1823	1836	1852	6			6	6
	1823	1836	dead					
1796	1828		1878	6	7		13	9
1792	1828		1859					
1820	1862							
1797	1828	1874	1877	8	25		33	23
1798	1828	1874	1881					
1810	1835		1883	4	12	2	18	15
1812	1835		1876					
1848								
1800	1832		1855	4	13	3	20	17
1808	1832							
	1820	1822	dead	1			1	1
	1820	1822	1882					
	1844	1848		4			4	2
	1844	1848	1857 dead					
1832	1877			2			2	2
1840	1877							
1809	1837	1851	1885	4	11		15	13
1810	1837	1853	1882					
1813	1837		1867	8	18		26	20
1809	1837							
1803	1828		1873	9	30	5	44	38
1804	1828		1872					
1794	1831		1859					
1792	1831		1879					
1814	1848		1854	4	8		12	9
1822	1848		1858					
1813	1837		1845					
1813	837		1874					
1801	1837	1841	1876	3	3		6	6

*Probably dead.

CATALOGUE, ALPHABETICALLY ARRANGED, OF THE
THE A. B. C. F. M. OF BOSTON. AND THE

Number of Reinforce.	NAMES OF MISSIONARIES.	PLACE OF BIRTH.
7	Lafon, Mrs. Sophia L. (Parker)	New Bedford, Mass
	Lafon, Mrs. Ruth A. (Atwell)	
7	Locke, Edwin	Fitzwilliam, N. H..
7	Locke, Mrs. Martha L. (Rowell)	Cornish, N. H
P	Loomis, Elisha	Middlesex, N. H...
P	Loomis, Mrs. Maria T. (Sartwell)	New Hartford,N.Y.
4	Lyman, Rev. David B	New Hartfo'd,Conn
4	Lyman, Mrs. Sarah (Joiner)	Royalton, Vt
4	Lyons, Rev. Lorenzo	oleraine, Mass....
4	Lyons, Mrs. Betsey (Curtis)	Elbridge, N. Y
7	Lyons, Mrs. Lucia G. (Smith)	Burlington, N. Y..
7	McDonald, Charles	Easton, Pa
7	McDenald, Mrs. Harriet (Halstead)	N. Y. City, N. Y..
7	Munn, Bethuel	Orange, N. J
7	Munn, Mrs. Louisa (Clark)	Skeneatles, N. Y..
	Munn, Mrs. (Bacon)	Clyde, N. Y
2	Ogden, Miss Maria	Philadelphia, Pa ..
8	Paris, Rev. John D	Stanton, Va
8	Paris, Mrs. Mary (Grant)	Albany, N. Y·
	Paris, Mrs. Mary (Carpenter)	N. Y. City, N. Y..
5	Parker, Rev. Benjamin W	Reading, Mass
5	Parker, Mrs. Mary E. (Barker)	Branford, Conn....
10	Pogue, Rev. John F	Wilmington, Del ..
10	*Pogue, Mrs. Maria K. (Whitney)	Waimea,Kauai,H.I.
8	Rice, William H	Oswego, N. Y
8	Rice, Mrs. Mary S. (Hyde)	Seneca Village,N.Y
1	Richards, Rev. William	Plainfield, Mass ...
1	Richards, Mrs. Clarissa (Lyman)	Northampton, Mass
4	Rogers, Edmund H	Newton, Mass
2	Rogers, Mrs. Mary (Ward)	Middlebury, N. Y..
6	Rogers, Mrs. Elizabeth (Hitchcock)	Gt.Barridgt'n,Mass
9	Rowell, Rev. George B	Cornish, N. H
9	Rowell, Mrs. Malvina J. (Chapin)	Newport, N. H
P	Ruggles, Samuel	Brookfield, Conn ..
P	Ruggles, Mrs. Nancy (Wells)	East Windsor,Conn
2	Shepherd, Stephen	Kingsboro, N. Y...

* Daughter of a missionary.

MISSIONARIES AT THE HAWAIIAN ISLANDS SENT BY SEAMENS' FRIEND SOCIETY OF N. Y.

Year of Birth	Year of Arrival	Date of Return	Date of Death	Number of Children	Number of Grand Ch'n	Great Gr'nd Children	Total Descendants	Dd'nts esc'n Living
1812	1837	1841	1844					
			1884					
1813	1837		1843	4	1		5	3
1812	1837		1842					
1799	1820	1827	1837					
1796	1820	1827	dead					
1803	1832		1884	8	37		45	38
1806	1832		1886					
1807	1832		1886	6	4		10	8
1813	1832		1837					
1810	1837							
1812	1837		1839					
1810	1837	1844		8	8		16	12
1803	1837	1841	1849	2			2	1
1810	1837		1841					
1792	1828		1874					
1809	1841			4	4		8	8
1807	1841		1847					
1815	1852							
1803	1833		1877	4	6		10	9
1805	1833							
1814	1844		1877					
1820	1844	1882						
1813	1841		1863	5	15		20	17
1813	1841							
1793	1823		1847	8	20		28	22
1794	1823	1849	1861					
1806	1832		1853	4	16		20	16
1799	1828		1834					
1802	1835		1857					
1815	1842		1884	7	27		34	28
1816	1842							
1795	1820	1834	1872	4			4	3
1791	1820	1834	1873					
1800	1828		1834	2			2	2

CATALOGUE, ALPHABETICALLY ARRANGED, OF THE THE A. B. C. F. M. OF BOSTON, AND THE

Number of Reinforce.	NAMES OF MISSIONARIES.	PLACE OF BIRTH.
2	Shepherd, Mrs. Margaret C. (Slow)..	Champion, N. Y...
13	Shipman, Rev. William C............	Wethersfield, Conn
13	Shipman, Jane (Stobie)..............	Aberdeen, Scotland
12	Smith, Rev. Asa B...................	Williamstown, Vt..
12	mith, Mrs. Sarah G. (White).......	W. Brookfield, Mass
9	Smith, Rev. J. W., M. D.............	Stamford, Conn....
9	Smith, Mrs. Melicent (Knapp).......	Greenwich, Conn..
5	Smith, Rev. Lowell..................	Heath, Mass.......
5	Smith, Mrs. Abba W. (Tenney).......	Barre, Mass.......
7	Smith, Miss Marcia M..............	Burlington, N. Y..
4	Spaulding, Rev. Ephraim............	Ludlow, Vt........
4	Spalding, Mrs. Julia (Brooks)........	Buckland, Mass ...
1	Stewart, Rev. Charles S.............	Flemington, N. J..
1	Stewart, Mrs. Harriet B.(Tiffany)....	Stamford, Conn....
	Taylor, Rev. T. E....................	
	*Taylor, Mrs Persis G. (Thurston)...	Kailua, H. I.......
P	Thurston, Rev. Asa..................	Fitchburg, Mass...
P	Thurston, Mrs. Lucy (Goodale)......	Marlboro, Mass....
3	Tinker, Rev. Reuben	Chester, ass......
3	Tinker, Mrs. Mary T. (Wood)........	Chester, Mass.....
7	Van Duzee, William S...............	Hartford, N. Y....
7	Van Duzee, Mrs. Oral (Hobart)......	Homer, N. Y ......
12	Wetmore, Dr. Charles H.............	Lebanon, Conn....
12	Wetmore, Mrs. Lucy S. (Taylor).....	Pittsfield, Mass...
P	Whitney, Rev. Samuel...............	Branford, Conn....
P	Whitney, Mrs. Mercy (Partridge)....	Pittsfield, Mass ...
10	Whittlesey, Rev. Eliphilat...........	Salisbury, Conn...
10	Whittlesey, Mrs. Elizab'th K.(Baldwin)	Frankfort, N. J...
7	Wilcox, Abner.......................	Harwinton, Conn..
7	Wilcox, Mrs. Lucy E. (Hart).........	Cairo, N. Y.......

* Daughter of a missionary.

174 Whole number of names in the table.
75 Men of these have families.
67 of these families have children, but 65 only are counted, as the children of Messrs. Pogue and Taylor are numbered in the descendants of Mr. Whitney and Thurston.

CATALOGUE, ALPHABETICALLY ARRANGED, OF THE
THE A. B C F: M. OF BOSTON, AND THE

Year of Birth.	Year of Arrival.	Date of Return.	Date of Death.	Number of Children.	Number of Grand Ch'n	Great Gr'nd Children.	Total Descendants.	Desc'nd'nts Living.
1801	1828		dead					
1824	1854		1861	3	6		9	7
1827	1854							
1809	1842	1845	1886					
1813	1842	1845						
1810	1843			9	17		26	22
1816	1843							
1802	1833			5	6		11	6
1809	1833		1885					
1806	1837	1852						
1802	1832	1836	1840	4	5		9	7
1810	1832	1836						
1798	1823	1825	1870	3	3		6	3
1798	1823	1825	1830					
	1843	1859	1883					
1821	1843	1861						
1787	1820		1868	5	18	8	31	22
1795	1820		1876					
1799	1 31	1840	1854	6			6	6
1809	1831	1840						
1811	1837	1840	1883	9	6		15	10
1814	1837	1840						
1820	1849			4	2		6	5
1819	1849		1883					
1793	1820		1845	4	15	6	25	19
1795	1820		1872					
1816	1844	1854						
1821	1844	1855						
1808	1837		1869	8	10		18	17
1814	1837		1869					

◉ NOTE EXPLANATORY OF THE TABLE.—This catalogue is designed to include the names of all the missionaries, both clergymen and laymen of the

A. B, C. F. M., except those sons born in the islands who are, or have been, in the field and work of their fathers. These are included in the number of the children of the original missionaries named in the table.

The sons who have labored under the American or Hawaiian Boards are the Messrs. Gulicks, S. E. Bishop, A. O. Forbes, H. H. Parker and H. Bingham. The Hawaiian Board and Micronesian and Marquesan Missions, are all out-growths of the American Board's Mission at the Hawaiian Islands. Messrs. Diell, Damon and Taylor, of the Seamen's Friend Society, and the Rev. William Ellis, of the London Missionary Society, are included in the table.

Of the descendants of the missionaries our data are incomplete, and the whole number is considerably larger than appears in the table. Four of the 75 families have no children. To three more, there are none credited, though some are known, and the others are believed to have them, but how many are not known. Whilst to 14 of the remaining families, the *known* descendants are credited, but they are also known to have *more, yet how many* is uncertain. The number of descendants of the remaining 54 families is pretty accurately ascertained.

There appears in the table 359 children, 694 grandchildren, and 48 great grandchildren, 1101 in all. Of these, 228 have died, leaving *apparently* 873 living descendants from the 66 families in the table having children credited to them; but there remains 68 who are twice counted, being the descendants of missionary children who have intermarried, and who appear in the table accredited to both grand parents. This reduces the living descendants as far as ascertained to 805.

The following names of ladies appear in the catalogue who have not resided at the Islands, but contracted marriage witn the missionaries named after they had left—to-wit: Mrs. Dr. S. L. Andrews, Mrs. H. Bingham, Mrs. D. T. Conde, Mrs. Wm. Ellis, Mrs. Dr. Lafon, the second and third Mrs. T. D. Hunts, and Mrs. Munn.

The *facts* in the "Review of the Mission Work" have been taken from the histories of Bingham, Dibble, Jarves and Anderson, and the table has been chiefly prepared from informatian collected from the members and publications of the Society and the "Maternal Association of the Mission."

MARY FRAZIER AND OTHER REMINISCENCES.

BY MRS. A. S. COOKE.

On the 14th of December, 1836, the barque Mary Frazier, Captain Charles Sumner, commander, left the city of Boston bound to the Sandwich Islands. She carried thirty-two passengers, who were expecting to spend their lives on those islands. They felt that they were called to go and dwell with those ignorant, degraded people, to teach them the way of life and happiness through Jesus Christ the Savior. With this in view they gladly bade farewell to relatives, friends, home and country. They were strangers to each other yet bound together by the strongest bonds and tenderest ties. As they left the harbor of Boston, a furious storm came on, and the first three days and nights were terrible to the seasick passengers, many of whom were never before on a ship. It seemed to them to threaten an end to their work before it was begun. There were several who did not recover when fair weather came. They made a specialty of seasickness, from which no remedy could decoy them.

The barque was well-fitted out for the long voyage. The necessary eatables were plentiful and good, and many luxuries also were provided, and kind friends had added extras to our stores.

The captain and officers were sk.l.ful, faithful, thoughtful and kind. The passengers were all young married people, excepting two.

Though unacquainted with each other they had

strong points of union. They had enlisted in the same company, under the same Master. They received their marching orders together. They were to go forward, not looking behind them. On reaching the field of battle, they were to reinforce the army in the field, loyal to their King, they were to carry the standard of truth and defend it from its enemies.

As the Mary Frazier company recovered from seasickness, they began to look around for work to do on the way. Some books were on board in the Hawaiian language; there were also two native seamen on the vessel named Joseph and Levi. Soon a class was formed to study their language. At certain times we were allowed the assistance of said Hawaiians to correct our pronunciation. We had a part of the New Testament, a few children's primers, and a pamphlet dictionary. The latter we prized highly, though it was incomplete and incorrect. There being *few* books, and many who wanted to study, great use was made of pencils and paper. Time did not seem long or hang heavy on our hands while on the Mary Frazier. Many books were read and many letters written. One of the company changed the dictionary from Hawaiian English to English Hawaiian. Then there was a rage for copying the work. Memory recalls those long days at sea as precious and delightful.

The captain gave permission for an evening gathering for prayers early on our voyage. He often attended and allowed officers and men to do so, when not on duty. These seasons become regular informal meetings.

The Lord heard the prayers and blessed the efforts of his children. They walked softly before Him in humility, using opportunities for private conversation and prayer with individuals. Joy filled our hearts when some of those who had never known the blessed Father, began to speak of His love to them and of their decision to accept the pardon offered to them in the Gospel. There was joy on the ship, and we all felt that there was joy among the angels in heaven over repenting souls.

Our voyage was prosperous in all respects. There was only that one storm. We doubled Cape Horn on the 60th day out. Our vessel anchored in the roadstead on the 116th day from Boston. It was on the Sabbath, and was an exciting day. The pilot came out to us, followed by some natives in canoes. The men on the latter were not clad. How shocked the ladies were! Some of them went down stairs and wept. They realized now that they had left the civilized world behind them. It was the island of Oahu that lay before us. As we gazed at it from the ship, it had a very dreary, uninteresting appearance. The city was not verdant as we see it to-day. Nuuanu valley was green, and there was what looked like green bushes on the sides of some mountains. The grass huts looked too small for human habitation. Scarce any foreign buildings were to be seen.

In the harbor were three small vessels and a barque, which the pilot told us was the King's vessel, recently purchased to take the remains of his sister Nahienaena to Lahaina for interment.

The entrance to the harbor was crooked and narrow, more so than it is now. Large vessels required help from men and boats to enter. The Mary Frazier was thus towed in Monday morning, April 10, 1837. The King sent his barge to bring us ashore. The first house we entered was the Hale Kauila. It belonged to the King. It was a large grass house near the sea, on the ground where Mr. Hackfield's store is now. We were there introduced to the young King Kauikeaouli, who welcomed us to his country gracefully and cordially—his speech was translated by the Rev. Hiram Bingham. An introduction to all the other chiefs followed. About twenty of these were present.

A young chief, three years of age, was asleep on the hikie. He was attended by servants waving kahilis over him. This was the young Prince Alexander Rihoriho, the King's adopted son.

While there, some of the company tried airing their knowledge of the Hawaiian language, much to the astonishment and amusement of those present. They were politely told that they were akamai loa.

It was very hot and dusty on shore. No rain had fallen during the winter. There was no grass and the dust was soft and deep in the paths. There were no real streets.

From this halealii we walked to the Mission, entering first the house of Rev. H. Bingham. Our captain accompanied us. Here we met all the missionaries then at the station. There were present: Mr. and Mrs. Bingham, Mr. and Mrs.

Lowell Smith, Mr. and Mrs. Tinker, Mr. and Mrs. Dimond, Dr. and Mrs. Judd, and Mr. and Mrs. Hall. There we all joined most heartily in devotional exercises appropriate to the occasion. Sincerely did we thank the Lord for his blessings to us while crossing the mighty oceans. After a few warm speeches of welcome, we were introduced to all our new brothers and sisters—were cordially received by them and adopted into the large family.

It did not take long to separate our company and locate us in the different families of the station. Rooms were improvised by curtains, so that all were soon made comfortable and felt at home. Mr. Cooke and myself were located with Mr. and Mrs. Dimond, who were special friends of his in New York city.

We often saw Capt. Sumner while he remained in port, and it was delightful to note the real change in him. In the first part of our voyage he caviled at the Bible and Christianity, and especially at Missions. He now took the Christian side. When we were at anchor on that first Sunday, he said, "I have been here before, and I see the difference. Formerly, as soon as my anchor was down, my ship was surrounded with men and women clamoring to come on board. How different now! It is Christianity that has caused the change!" When on shore, he took the part of the missionaries on all occasions, when with their enemies or traducers.

"Oh, you need not tell me these stories," he said to them, "I have lived four months with these dreadful people and know them well. I know the *natives*, too, as they were many years ago, and I am fully convinced that the change I see is from the influence of the religion of the Bible." Mr. Brinsmade, whom you all remember, told us these and many other things of our captain which we were glad to know.

Before Captain Sumner left Honolulu, he wished to leave his testimony on record. He therefore made a profession of his faith in the Savior. He wanted, he said, "to join the great Church of Christ—the Church Universal." The second mate of the vessel and four of the seamen also joined the Church at the same time. The exercises were at the Bethel. Rev. Mr. Diel was the pastor. While the vessel was in port a series of meetings were held in English for seamen and others. The captain and his men attended and took an active part.

We found on our arrival that there was much interest in the subject of religion here in Honolulu among the natives. The great revival of 1837–8 had commenced, and meetings were well attended. At daylight the bell rang, and natives, men, women and children, went to the house of prayer. Protracted meetings had been held in some places. The people went to the houses of their teachers for personal conversation. They wished to tell their *manao* to the pastor. Their thoughts were very similar. They had been great sinners, they said, broken all God's commandments, enumerating them one by one, now they wished to turn from sin and serve the living God. It almost seemed as if some of them had learned the words as a lesson to be recited, as they were sometimes prompted by friends when memory failed them. They took the name of *hooikaikas*, which word means perseverers, and they meant that they would persevere in the right way. The *pono* was popular. The chiefs favored it and gave their influence for it. This condition of things made it difficult to distinguish between the chaff and the wheat.

Rev. Lowell Smith lived in Honolulu, and had charge of the schools when we arrived. Mr. Cooke and myself commenced attending his school the second week after our arrival, and we were gratified to find that we could take a part. We could teach classes in reading, writing and arithmetic. It assisted us in learning native character, and especially in getting the language. It was our private opinion that we made greater progress than our pupils did.

Mr. Cooke was not a minister, but he had an honest, earnest desire to help in spreading the good news of the Gospel among these people and he was willing to work in any way for this end. He came out here as a *teacher*. His occupation at home was mercantile. But, attending meetings for natives or foreigners, distributing tracts, visiting from house to house, or any kind of work to do good, was prized by him as a golden opportunity to be improved if possible.

The *General Meeting* was a great event in those days. It was the yearly gathering of all the missionaries from all the islands, in Honolulu. In some respects it was like the Jews going up to Jerusalem. It was a general vacation. Many came from places so isolated that a white face was seldom seen. The families needed the change. They needed it socially and mentally, as well as spiritually. It was specially needed for mutual counsel and encouragement in the work. This gathering took place earlier than usual this year, because of the arrival of our larger company.

We gladly made the acquaintance of those of whom we had so often read and almost envied, before coming to this country. While together, a kind of Mission parliament was held every week day.

The place of meeting was the adobe school house, still standing near the Kawaiahao Church. Both gentlemen and ladies attended. The children also came with their parents. Fathers often made speeches with little children in their arms, and the infants did sometimes interrupt the grave discussions by expressing independent ideas on foreign subjects. The boys who inherited the whittling propensity left interesting and still visible evidence of their industry and undeveloped genius in the art of sculpture. Those benches stand in the yard outside of the building now, the artistic work not being appreciated by the present generation. Some of those young sculptors are grand parents now; they doubtless look back to those days with interest and pleasure.

The subject of location was one of great importance to all, for changes were often made on account of health and for other reasons. The new comers were especially interested in this subject.

From every station reports were read. They

told of work accomplished and work to be done, of success and discouragements, of meetings, schools, of need of finances and need of helpers. This was all very interesting. We shall never forget Mr. Lyon's reports. They were long, full of interesting episodes, with touches of humor—a great deal of good sense and evidence of a large heart full of love for his work and energy in doing it.

The subject of finance was one of general interest and much perplexity. Funds for the work all came from Boston—were limited and must be used with care and wisdom. Government did not then build school houses or pay teachers. Missionaries did not have salaries, but were supported on the common stock basis. Now, after seventeen years experience, many began to feel that this unbusiness-like way was uneconomical and injurious to the individuals and all concerned. The subject was discussed but not settled. Permission was, however, given to any who so desired to draw a salary of $400 a year for a man and his wife.

A school for the children of the Mission was a subject of general interest. Parents felt keenly on this subject. Overwhelmed themselves with Mission work, they had no time to educate their children. Messrs. Tireman and Bennett, when here, warned parents against native influence, advising them not to allow the children to converse with the natives at all. Those who went from these Islands to Tahiti noticed the *dreadful effect, the deadly blight* on children of missionaries growing up among the natives there. From these representations resulted the almost universal tabu of the native language to the children of missionaries here on these islands. Many parents felt that their children must not be kept in this land after they were six years old. Some were sent to friends at home, but the long journey was objectionable and the separation painful and unnatural. After long discussion and earnest seeking for special guidance, it was decided. There must be a school for Mission children *here*. The Rev. Hiram Bingham generously gave the land for that purpose. The school prospered. It is now in existence, and is called *Oahu College*. The children of the missionaries have passed on, but many of their grandchildren occupy their places, and are fitting for spheres of usefulness.

During this General Meeting (the one of 1837), Rev. Lowell Smith was appointed to take a new parish in the lower part of the town called Kaumakapil. He commenced to build, and in course of the year had erected a dwelling house and school house. Mr. Cooke was directed to take Mr. Smith's place in the schools, though the former continued to teach while superintending the building at Kaumakapili. Mr. Cooke and myself both taught in the schools at Kawaiahao, and all the outside schools were visited often. All the schools came together on the Sabbath at Kawaiahao. About three hundred were usually present. Others at the station rendered assistance in the Sabbath school.

During the General Meeting of 1839, the King and chiefs sent a request for a teacher to be set apart for their children, naming Mr. Cooke as the one whom they had selected. They sent *him* a letter also. On being consulted, Mr. Cooke replied that we felt unequal to such a position, and would not consider it a wise appointment. Our objections were overruled and we undertook the work, though with many misgivings.

For one year the pupils came daily to our house for instruction. Their servants came with them, about forty in number lounging about the grounds while the pupils were in school, a hindrance to the pupils and an annoyance to the teachers. The school building was erected during the year, but it was not ready for occupation till April, 1840.

It was a very trying time when the day came to separate these young children from their parents and kahus. There were sad faces and many tears. The number of scholars was sixteen, not counting a few foreign children who came as day scholars. When we commenced, our eldest pupil was thirteen, and the youngest was less than two years old. Only three of the sixteen are now living. Four of them have been kings, one a queen, and one is now heir apparent.

A thorough knowledge of the English language was thought desirable in this school, both as colloquial and written. Therefore all the books used in the school were in the English tongue. In this language we taught the sciences, giving them the keys that unlocked the citadels of knowledge, that they might understand the word and works of God. We taught also of man, of his body and soul, of the importance of his life here. Of the great good Father, and what He required of His children. Of the consequences of disobedience to his laws and of the beautiful home made ready for all those who loved, obeyed and trusted in his son Jesus Christ.

Hon. John Ii and his wife were with us all the time we spent in the school. They were a help and comfort to us. We always found them on the side of good government, good order and goodness generally.

Mr. Richards, Dr. G. P. Judd and Mr. Armstrong gave us constant encouragement. They lent us their influence and all the help that they could render from the positions that they occupied as government officers.

Mr. Richard gave a course of lectures to the King and chiefs on the science of government, to which the elder members of our school were invited. He also gave a series of lectures on his return from Europe, descriptive of places, people and customs of other countries.

Mr. Armstrong preached Sunday evenings at the palace before the King and chiefs on subjects adapted especially to rulers—to the times—and to *Hawaii nei*.

We had assistance, some of the time, from able teachers, among whom I would name Prof. C. S. Lyman and Rev. J. Douglas.

But I must not weary you. I will only say with reference to ourselves—that this work was not of our own selection. It was arduous and full of difficulties, many of which I do not wish to recall. We had foes without our walls, and, like the garden of Eden, the serpent was on the watch and would sometimes find a way inside and work to do.

What was given us to do in that school we tried to do faithfully, not sparing ourselves and not forgetting our responsibility to the King of kings.

We remained in the school till 1850. Three of the eldest girls were married. The young Princes were travelling in Europe with Dr. G. P. Judd. The school was disbanded.

The *results* of our work are not all known in this world, but they will be known in the hereafter.

There is a wide difference between the spirit of heathenism and the spirit of the Gospel. The former teaches selfishness. Its tender mercies are cruel. The delicate infant is strangled by its own parents. Helpless aged people are buried alive. Woman is treated as an *inferior*, enslaved and abused. The spirit of the Gospel teaches love and kindness to all, even to *enemies*. It builds hospitals for the sick poor, giving them care, kindness and medical aid. It builds homes for the aged who have no friends to care for them, smoothing their pathway and comforting them with the hope and blessings ready for them in the home above. It builds and supports schools for the children, causing them to be taught and developed into noble men and women, an honor to their country, an influence for good, and a blessing to the world.

Let us recognize in the Queen's Hospital, the Lunalilo Home for the aged poor, and the noble provision for the Kamehameha Schools some of the beneficent fruits of the Gospel of our Lord and Savior, left us as precious mementos of *some, whose faces we shall see no more on earth,* and who were members of the Chiefs' Children's School.

———o———

MEMORIALS OF THE REINFORCEMENT OF 1837.

BY MRS. LUCIA G. LYONS.

To the remnant of the "Mary Frazier Company," assembled at Honolulu with their children, greeting:

Fifty years ago to-day a company of thirty-two who had been four months at sea, were nearing Hawaii, with varied feelings of hope and fear. Of hope, that they might do much to aid a nation to rise in the scale of comfort, intelligence and Christianity. Of fear, lest the qualifications for the work were sadly defective. Nor had they longer to wait for the test; for April 9th took them into Honolulu harbor on the Sabbath.

The next day we all went ashore, and as we walked from the landing to the old mission premises, then occupied by Father Bingham, through a crowd of half-naked men, women and children, there seemed evidence of plenty of work for the weakest of our company. On the part of the laborers already on the field we had a cordial welcome. I remember the hearty words of Father Bishop, ending with, "We did not expect to see you so soon, or so many of you, or so cheery a company."

And I should like to know how many of that company felt the lifting power of Rev. Mr. Tinker's address one evening to the new comers, in that large room of the Chamberlain house, then used for religious meetings,—on the words, "the Lord hath need of him?" He told us how the Mission sent for teachers, of the great work to be done, and added in his own inimitable way "And you have well done that you have come." His words sound in my ears yet, though it is long since he rested from his labors.

Word and schooners were sent to the other islands, and the assembled mission—after much deliberation and many changes of plan—had the whole thirty located, and those for the other islands were soon on their way thither.

Father Castle's work was ready to his hand from the first day of our arrival, and Honolulu has been his home all these fifty years, work varying, but hands, mind and heart ever full. While she, who left home with him, the picture of health, fainted and fell by the way, loved and lamented, but safe at home. Her little one, so soon left motherless, has grown, I hear, to belong to one of the giant class, along with her large family of sons and daughters.

Angeline's place was filled by one who has borne her full share of the work implied in keeping an open house for multitudes, while bringing up those stalwart men and women who are an honor to their parents. From sharing their hospitality often, I know more of their children than of any other family.

But let us follow others to their fields of labor. Six men and their wives were sent to Hawaii. Mr. Van Duzee, teacher, was with Rev. Cochran Forbes at Kealakekua; Dr. Andrews, M.D., with Father Thurston at Kailua, in Mr. Bishop's old house. Rev. Mr. Bliss, and Mr. Bailey, teacher, were the first resident missionaries of North Kohala; Mr. Knapp, teacher at Waimea, South Kohala, and Mr. Wilcox, teacher at Hilo, and all got to work during the year.

Not one of these twelve individuals is left on Hawaii, and but four on earth. Brother and Sister Bailey on Maui, Dr. Andrews in Michigan, and Mrs. Van Duzee in New York. And of seventeen sons in these families (am I correct in the number?) not one is a missionary or preacher, that I know of. There are two female missionaries from the small number of girls; but both in Persia. Of these seventeen sons, I have seen but eight, but I hear of them as active business men. Can they not combine, and originate and carry out a plan of labor that will save some of the natives fast going back to heathenism, and some of other nationalities congregated on the sugar plantations, and in the rice fields? Would not some souls saved be worth more than hoarded gold?

Of this group first sent to Hawaii, remains the only couple unbroken of our company: Brother and Sister Bailey. Accept, dear brother and sister, my congratulations on the completion of this full half century of united life and labor. You are left the sole representatives of the Mary Frazier's company on Maui. When you came to Hawaii, our loved brother, Mr. McDonald, was stationed at Lahaina *lalo*. How soon his race was run! His wife, long a widow for the second time, has some claims on us more favored ones. I told her she ought to let us know some particulars of her circumstances. But to return.

Rev. Messrs. Ives and Conde were sent to Hana, a new station. All these sleep the sleep of the just except Mr. Conde. One son of Mr. Ives is a preacher, and two daughters, teachers. One son of Mr. Conde is a preacher, and one daughter a teacher, and all appear to be useful citizens.

My station, too, was Maui, so fixed before I left home. But I did not reach Lahainaluna till the latter part of August, and at the end of ten months, I took this more permanent station without asking leave of the Mission. The rest you know, something as I know the history and experience of the rest of the company.

But this was not all of our company. Brother and Sister Munn were sent to Molokai. She was a cherished friend, and prized correspondent, but four years finished her work. I saw her but once after I came to Hawaii. He soon followed, and it is cause for regret that we know nothing of their two sons.

Brother Johnson went to Kauai, which in those days seemed often farther from us in many respects than the Eastern States are now. And I have not seen Sister Johnson but once since they sailed for Kauai in 1837. Her husband, one of the youngest of our company, has long rested on Ebon, while the waves of sorrow have been borne by her alone. Oh no, not alone, for is she not one to whom Jesus says, "Lo I am with you always?"

Kauai had another treasure for a few years, in our brother, Rev. Dr. Lafon. I did not see him after 1839, but his memory is precious. The Lord bless their children. These two families were all who went to Kauai, but the Mission children of our company, now there, are sons of the one sent to Hilo, then the most southern station on Hawaii.

Let us return to Oahu. This, from Kauai, would take a week, perhaps longer. Here we find our brother Edwin Locke and his wife, with characteristic energy and enthusiasm, entering into the work of a boys' boarding school. But alas, how short their day of work here! I have copied a few lines written by him, on a separate paper. Some may like to recall him thus to remembrance.

One more couple remains: Amos S. Cooke and wife, and they were left in Honolulu, included, so to say, in the circle forming "Castle and Cooke." But what this implies was not their first work. They commenced as teachers, and became the teachers of kings, queens and princes. A trying post, with severe labor, patiently performed, in some of the fruits of which they still rejoice. Do I err to say *they*, though one is beyond our sight? The Lord bless the children who live to care for their mother, and give her a mother's greatest joy.

Those who remain, and are together, I greet with a hearty aloha. Not counterfeit, but true coin. Aloha, aloha nui, a mau.

Part 2. To any who have any interest in the matter:

It was not my intention to say anything about my work. Perhaps a few facts may be admissible. I was sent out as a teacher for the wives of the married scholars at Lahainaluna. Before we arrived, the Mission had decided to receive no more adult scholars. Thus I was met at the threshold of mission life with, "Your work is *pau*." I went to Lahaina, however, and taught what wives there were there, and about twenty native children. I had a school, also, half a day for the children of Messrs. Clark, Andrews and Dibble.

When I arrived in Waimea, the 18th of July, 1838, I commenced teaching at once, persons that were the first children ever gathered into a school in Waimea. But the older class had been in school two years or more. Of the oldest class of girls, one remains, a feeble, white-haired woman, and a consistent Christian. Of the second class, I know of but one, the grandmother of a married woman. Of the third class, Mrs. Hon. John Parker alone remains in Waimea. Of the bright boys of the older class, children of George Davis, and others, all are gone from earth. Of younger ones, Judge Hoapili, of Kona, remains, and one other in Waipio. The local magistrate of Waimea was then learning his letters. I took his sister to live with us very soon and kept her ten years. Some years later I took the mother of Curtis Iaukea, who lived with us most of the time till she married Mr. Iaukea. Her memory is dear, for hers was a life-long friendship. All of that company of girl boarders are gone. I do not remember how many there were.

The next experiment was to take children into the family, and have them sit at the table with us, and in every respect they worked and studied and lived as our own children. Of these, we had twenty in all, mostly girls. Some staid eleven or twelve years; other six and seven, some four, and one, one year. Many of these are living. For many years we had a day school, of which these boarding scholars were part. These day scholars are now married men and women, with families of their own. Our last boarders left us in 1879, and my throat then had a much needed rest from teaching. These last boarders were grandchildren of one of the first class of girls I took.

Since October, 1879, I had rested from teaching except in Sunday School, until January, of this year, 1887. Am now teaching twenty of the youngest scholars in the district school, mostly children of people who were born after I came to Waimea.

Would you like know why I gave so much of my time to teaching? Partly because it was the only thing I could carry out, in our circumstances.

A word from Brother Edwin Locke, not from the spirit land, through a medium, but a copy of what he penned on board the Mary Frazier off Cape Horn, February 25, 1837:

"A sound was heard in the land of the Pilgrim Fathers. It came from the abodes of darkness, and the habitations of cruelty. From the four quarters of the world, and the isles of the sea, it came to the home of the Christian. 'Twas not like the thunder of heaven, nor the whirlwind of earth, nor like the still, small voice, which spake to the prophet.

"But it was the sound of misery, wretchedness, sorrow and anguish, caused by ignorance, superstition and sin. With it came the supplication and entreaty, 'Send me the Book of books. Send me Jesus Christ's man. Oh, send me one, to tell about the white man's God.' And sister, hast thou listened to that cry, and in obedience to 'thy Savior's last command' left thy native land' to relieve that misery and wretchedness; and to point the sinner to that fountain, in which if they wash they shall be clean. Then heed not the world, whatever its course. Some will impeach your motives, and others sneer at your philanthropy, and scorn your pity, while they laugh at your folly. He who said, 'In the world ye shall have tribulation,' also said 'Lo I am with you always, even to the end of the world.'"

———o———

THE SCHOOLMASTER IN HAWAII.

BY EDWARD BAILEY.

Every true servant of God waits ready to do his will when it is made known to him.

He may misapprehend the message in its applicability to himself; he may misjudge his own fitness to fill any particular sphere, though the will is ready to perform the duty which is supposed to be known. But it is often only on trial that the fitness or unfitness of a proposed instrument becomes fully apparent, and is found to be useful or otherwise.

The character and wants of the Sandwich Island missionary field were chiefly known to the religious world through the A. B. C. F. M., and they laid them before the Christian community mostly in the pages of the "Missionary Herald."

Thus we who came to the work in the reinforcement, which sailed from Boston, on the 14th of December, 1836, understood that the field was most invitingly open, and the missionaries already on the ground were urgently calling for help. An intense desire to be taught had been awakened, and it became an urgent need that the untutored people be educated. They had almost everything worth knowing yet to learn.

The mission spirit at home was at its zenith. Consecration was the great watchword among Christians. And by those truly devoted a fitness to occupy in any capacity some mission field was desired, and the privilege to do so was eagerly sought.

In this spirit we sailed for the Islands on board the dear old Mary Frazier. During the voyage our company of thirty-two became acquainted with each other; and the little idiosyncrasies of each became more or less fully known.

Prayer and praise, and mission work among the crew were the exercises by which the missionary muscle was tested.

But some suffered as well; and in two cases there is reason to think the foundation was laid for an early death. I refer to Sister Lafon and Brother MacDonald.

In due time the field was before our own eyes; and we were able to judge for ourselves, though great anxiety had been expressed lest we be too independent in making our own estimate of things; and very solemn admonitions had been given that we do not seem to disagree with what had already been put before the world.

I can say with truth that I was very slow in making up my mind as to what had been done; but I was far more clear in relation to what was to be done.

But we were destined to enter on our station with more experience than might have been the case, though a delay of a few weeks was somewhat of a damper to our zeal to commence work at once. We were to be located at the new station of Kohala, in company with Rev. Isaac Bliss and wife. His sickness delayed us; and finally I was on the ground to reside sometime before him. While we awaited his convalescence we went to Kaneohe, and spent a few weeks very pleasantly and profitably with those devoted model missionaries, Brother and Sister Parker. I think the lessons we took from them were not in vain.

When we had reached our ultimate destination we took hold of our work honestly and zealously. That faithful and unselfish missionary, Rev. Lorenzo Lyons, at whose house we tarried a little on our way, introduced us to our work and helped us in many ways.

The great questionings about the missionary life were now answered in part, and we were not disappointed. Many a bugbear had vanished into thin air. Our dreams were happily realized. Every effort would tell. We were never lonesome; the people flocked around us in crowds, and seemed to drink in with avidity all we could give them. As far as possible, in such different conditions, we were in sympathy with them. Mr. Lyons came over from Waimea and gave us the keynote to our work. He had just lost his dear wife, a sister of Mrs. Bliss, and was in great affliction, but the Master's work was not allowed to delay, and he followed on to the end of his long life, devoid of self-seeking, but pouring out his large heart for the welfare of the Hawaiians. Our entrance to the work was at the beginning of one of the greatest outpourings of God's Spirit in modern times.

My own proper work as teacher was very much blended with that of the preacher, as, at the request of Mr. Bliss, I did nearly all the preaching at first; he finding it very difficult to get such a knowledge of the language as to enable him to do it intelligibly. Thousands crowded the immense grass church which we found already built.

But children also swarmed thick as bees, and I felt very desirous to get about my own proper work. From the first, I had a school of teachers; poor as they were, they were the best to be had. But schools there must be; and, though it seemed somewhat incongruous to put men of forty or more through the child's arithmetic, it was necessary.

But something higher must be aimed at, and a selection was made of the brightest boys for a class to be under my constant care and training. A good beginning was made, but some obstacles arose of a nature to greatly interfere with the work, and with great reluctance, I was obliged to abandon it for the time being.—I mean the class of boys.

Though heathenism was nominally abolished, how deeply its corrupting influences had pervaded the whole fibre of the race.

Our residence in Kohala was short, only about two years. At the end of that time we were placed at Lahainaluna to partly fill the place of Rev. E. W. Clark, who made a visit to China for his health, and of Rev. Sheldon Dibble, absent for similar reasons in the United States.

It may seem strange, but it was a fact that after living so long as we had lived in grass houses with floors of mats laid upon grass or ferns, which required us to raised the foot high in stepping, we at first raised the foot higher than was necessary in stepping on floors of board, few of the mission houses being matted at that time. The whole paraphernalia of civilization seemed awkward after living so long in great simplicity. We had a painful sense that now we were backwoodsmen.

At Lahainaluna we had entered on a work of peculiar importance. The future men of influence, so far as natives were concerned, were here being trained. But my work was confined mostly to the secular affairs of the school, and at the end of one year Messr. Dibble and Clark having returned, the Mission voted us back to Kohala, with the privilege of taking a new station if we wished it. This plan—doubtfully proposed, was not carried out. By the advice of the missionaries at Lahaina, and some from Hawaii on their way home from General Meeting, we remained on Maui, and finally located at Wailuku with Rev. J. S. Green. Rev. Richard Armstrong was called to Honolulu to take the place of Rev. Hiram Bingham, who left for the United States finally as it proved.

Good work had been done at Wailuku by Brethren Richards, Tinker, Green and Armstrong.

But I must here say that, unless for very good reasons a missionary whose ideals are formed for his first field, should not be removed therefrom. Those ideals were not then impossible of accomplishment, and if they had been fully carried out, Hawaii would to-day have been a vastly different place from what it is.

The people, as a whole, or especially as individuals could not be made to feel responsibility. Their chiefs did so and so, and that was all there was of it in their estimation.

Christianity seemed firmly established at Wailuku; there was a large and flourishing church, and some faint glimmerings of the dawn of civilization.

We entered with zeal on our work; a selection was made of all the brightest and most hopeful boys on Maui for my school, and for one happy year I taught them Colburn's "First Lessons" being the center of the reasoning radius whence the branches spread to infinity. This was my happiest missionary year, and in its results, most satisfactory.

But Brother Green who had established the Wailuku Female Seminary, wishing to devote himself wholly to ministerial work, the charge of the Seminary devolved on me and remained in my hands for eight years, 1841–48.

Miss Ogden was our faithful and devoted fellow-laborer. It was an arduous work; none without experience can realize how much so, and how constant was the weight of care. But it was a glorious work; and a last hope for the Hawaiian race, fast verging toward a state of helplessness.

But as it became apparent that not all looked upon it in that light I became despondent; and when the Board wished to put the Mission on a self-supporting basis, and no such basis being possible for the school, I did not greatly oppose when the Mission decided that the school be discontinued. That step of the Mission was a great mistake, as all acknowledged afterward. It happened in 1848.

I must say here that events have not fully justified my apprehensions. Much good was done.

Hitherto, without any medical education whatever, I was practically the physician of whatever station I occupied, except Lahainaluna. In times when epidemics were prevalent we were much occupied in that way, and I really think we did the best we could.

For what reason I know not, the feeling, always present, that the missionary was not complete as a man, grew upon me and prepared me, more more readily than I might otherwise have done to comply with the wishes of the A. B. C. F. M., in seeking a support independently of them. Not that I looked upon their measure as a wise one, or that I now would approve of it. The missionary status had become too much a sui generis affair; when it should be the status of every one who professes to serve the Lord Jesus. At any rate that kind of missionary prestige was essentially weakened by the course of the Board. And the event put things in a false light, and justified the doubt with which it was received.

And now a new life was begun; success or defeat would depend on my own exertions; and money making—the taste for which was left out of my make up, was to be the way to a support for myself and family. I was not alone; several others left the Board at the same time, but, so far as I know, I was the only one who did not afterwards receive help again. I did not succeed in money-making except to a very small extent; and should be penniless to-day if my sons had not helped me.

As a conclusion, I will say that the questions,

always before me, remain yet unanswered, viz:
1. Is the world to be converted?
2. Wherein will that conversion consist?
3. What would be the present condition of the Hawaiian Islands had it been left for commerce to convert them?
4. Has the power acquired by the people through civilization and Christianity been used by them more for good or evil?
5. Does true manliness exist in the Hawaiian race to the extent we hoped?
6. Are rulers who are a terror to good works instead of evil works rulers at all in the Scriptural sense?

THE WORK OF REV. EDWARD JOHNSON.

Rev Edward Johnson was born in Hollis, New Hampshire. At an early age he decided to consecrate all his powers to the Master's service; for some time it was a question in his mind whether to labor as a home missionary among the Indians or to go out to a foreign field. Becoming interested in the work that had already begun in the Sandwich Islands, he decided to leave all the hallowed associations of his father-land and go out to these isles of the sea.

He completed his studies at Andover, Mass., was married Nov., 1836, to Miss Lois Hoyt, of Warner, New Hampshire, and set sail from Boston, Dec. 14th, on the bark Mary Frazier, together with a large band earnest men and women. After a prosperous voyage of one hundred and sixteen days they arrived at Honolulu, April 9th, 1837, just fifty years ago. Soon after their arrival, the Mission held their annual meeting, and Mr. Johnson was appointed to his station at Waiole, Island of Kauai, where he immediately commenced his labors as a teacher, while Mrs. Johnson formed a school for women and young girls, teaching them to read and sew. This she continued for several years. Although her time was fully occupied with cares and labors incident to pioneer missionary life, she was untiring in her efforts to instill precepts of love and order into the minds of her dark sisters, and in after years it was her privilege to see many of them holding useful positions as wives and mothers.

In 1848, Mr. Johnson was ordained to the ministry, the exercises taking place in the Kawaiahao Church. At this place on the same day occurred the marriage of Rev. J. F. Pogue to Miss Maria Whitney. Mr. Johnson's pastorate extended over an area of thirty miles, a portion of this was accessable only by sea, or over a narrow path leading around dizzy cliffs. He was untiring in his labors, and often went beyond his strength. In 1855, his health requiring change, he received leave of absence for a visit to his native land, arriving at home, just in time to see his aged father ere he passed away. He returned to the Islands in 1856. In 1867, he was appointed as delegate from the Hawaiian Mission to Micronesia, from whence he never returned; after a short illness, he passed away on board the "Morning Star," and was laid to rest on Mission soil at Ebon to await the summons, "Well done good and faithful servant, enter thou into the joy of thy Lord."

---o---

LIFE AT HANA.

BY REV. D. T. CONDE.

It was about the 14th of December, 1836, that we as members of a large company of recently installed missionaries and assistant missionaries, embarked for our destination, then called Sandwich Islands.

After recovering from seasickness, from which but few were exempted, we all commenced earnest efforts to promote the spiritual condition of the sailors and their commander as we were kindly permitted to do. The divine blessing was evidently vouchsafed. The captain, his first mate and several of the sailors were hopefully converted, made repeated confessions publicly, and engaged fervently in the good work. On arriving at the islands, these men, including the captain, united with the church.

On the arrival of our bark at Honolulu, we were conducted by Mr. Bingham to the Palace, to be presented to King Kamehameha III, by name Kauikeaouli, a gentlemen of ordinary size, and dressed in English costume, and of graceful manners. He received us kindly, being introduced individually by Mr. Bingham, and welcomed us into his Kingdom, promising protection and wishing us God speed in all lawful measures which we inaugurate tonight evangelize his people. The King was attended by several of his principal chiefs of both sexes. They, unlike himself, were persons of immense physique, especially the women. The latter lay sprawling upon a raised platform of sufficient dimensions, covered with mats. We thought them wonderful specimens of humanity—never before seen in all our range of observation. The royal palace, we noticed, was a *very* humble domicile, compared with that the present King probably occupies. It was built of posts and rafters, the former set in the ground, and the whole thatched with grass, from the ground to the top, not lined inside with anything. The floor was the ground, with a mat covering. Very little furniture to be seen; not even a throne, unless the modest sofa from which His Majesty rose when we appeared before him, could have been called one. The room, however, was very spacious and airy; and the whole structure including the environs, not only suitable but elegant for the times.

Presently the mission families had gathered for business. One of the first items of importance was to make a wise and satisfactory disposition of the new accession to their numbers, by designating each couple of the reinforcement, just arrived to some field of labor.

We, myself and wife, were commissioned to form a station on the eastern extremity of Maui, in the district of Hana and include that of Kipahula and Kaupo on the south, and Koolau on the north, altogether containing a pupulation of about 3,000.

Making our first trial of a Hawaiian coaster, on our way we disembarked at Lahaina with the view of tarrying there some four or five months, and pursuing the study of the language—wishing to become possessed of at least a partial knowledge thereof before going on to our field. Dr. Baldwin was the resident missionary at Lahaina, and was of great service to us on that occasion, and was always after a generous and excellent friend. Having completed our allotted time at Lahaina, we started for the scene of toil and sacrifice, for subsequent experience proved it to be such. We took passage on board the somewhat noted Hooikaika, one of the best of native schooners. We found it, however, filthy and crowded with filthy men and women from stem to stern. Were two days and one night in making the little harbor of Hana. We got ashore as soon as possible and with feeble steps made for the house put up by the people for our use, taking with us a mattress of dried grass, upon which we had reclined on deck, all the voyage. This mattress or bed was taken up by the people (for a large multitude had collected to welcome our arrival) and spread on the floor, where my wife with her first born three months old, lay down to rest. We found the house a mere shell. It was thatched with grass and not with much care. It had one puka only and was without a pani, this the only place of ingress and egress. A ground floor, spread with lauhala mats, soft and springy under foot. After getting the dear mother and precious babe (both objects of curiosity and tender solicitude, especially to the native women) comfortably retired upon their kahi moe, a uhuiia i ke kapa, food of various kinds was soon forth coming to satisfy appetites, sharpened by the fast of two days on board ship.

That first night at our new home, amid a heathen people, but friendly and sympathizing, we all slept safely and sweetly, for God's banner over us was love, we recognized that He was already giving us favor in the sight of the people and felt encouraged that success would ensue.

When the morning arrived it was holy time, the Lord's day. A large concourse assembled at 10 o'clock filling nearly the whole luakini for a large house of worship had, previously been erected of lauhala thatch, 130 ft. long by 30 ft. in width, the ground floor strewed with smooth, round pebbles, two or three inches deep, gathered from the ocean beach, near by. The congregation of men, women and children, with their scanty covering of native kapa, all squatted down tailor fashion, the two sexes separated, occupying either end of the house with a space between leading up to where their speaker was expected to stand— such the temple, in which, and such the first audience to which I delivered, or raather read, my first Hawaiian discourse.

The audience with upturned faces seemed to listen with close attention. But it is more than doubtful whether they apprehended any thing of the subject.

Some being questioned, characteristically replied, "Ua lohe no a ua hoomaopopo hoi, aka ua pohihihi nae."

As time advanced, my acquaintance with Hawaiian gradually matured, and the people composing my audience gradually acquired ability to understand and appreciate what I endeavored to teach them. Their place of habitation being so remote, so isolated and difficult of access, they could have but little intercourse with other localities more favorably situated as to civil and moral culture; hence, they all without exception, seemed profoundly ignorant; their intellects exceedingly obtuse, and as to moral sense they seemed quite destitute of it. Their homes too were mere hovels thatched with grass, low, contracted and filthy. They lived mostly in a nude state, and when otherwise, it was to throw over their shoulders a sheet or sheets of common kapa. Not a garment of foreign manufacture was worn by male or female—poor, supremely poor and degraded, both as to mind and body. But they were very approachable, kind and tractable. In beginning our operations among them, we treated them, of course, to first principles—the very alphabet of Christianity and civilization, and this we proceeded to do with earnestness and perseverance, as soon as we had settled ourselves, as a family, in tolerably comfortable circumstances.

As already hinted, a grass or lauhala thatched house had been put up for us about 12 by 20 ft., without doors or windows—merely an open place in one side to get into it, and with only a ground floor. I went to work myself and made two doors and as many windows and set them in position, and divided the house into two rooms by a mat partition—one for a sitting and sleeping apartment, the other to take our frugal meals in, also to receive callers in. The former I floored with loose rough boards and carpeted it with coarse native mats. After tastefully arranging our various articles of furniture brought with us from Boston, bureau, table, stand, bedstead, etc., and a few chairs (of course a rocking chair was one of them) our front seemed pleasant and homelike. For a kitchen or hale kuki, we used a small building situated a little distance from the dwelling house. Thus completed and adorned, our home, especially the interior was much admired and complimented by the people. They came from all quarters, in multitudes to see their kumus. They would crowd and lean against our house in such numbers and with so much force as nearly to crush in its sides, darken the windows with their faces peering in to get a glimpse of the wahine haori and keiki.

We would admit them into the reception room in companies of eight or ten, detain them a few minutes with an address about the man Christ—Savior of the soul—when they would retire and another similar company would come in and be treated in like manner. A part of almost every day for weeks this practice was observed. The religious awakening was general through our field and continued at intervals for years. We felt a corresponding inspiration and strove for a familiar acquaintance with the language that we might disseminate the good seed through the length and breadth of the country in a season so opportune. Schools were opened for the education of children and adults, in all suitable places, as fast as teachers could be procured, preferring such as were trained and fitted at the Lahainaluna Seminary. School houses were furnished by the people, by order of the Governor of the island. These buildings were also utilized for religious meetings, when the missionary made tours through the several districts for preaching, which occurred at least once a month, consuming usually a whole week, including the Sabbath. The people also took the liberty to hold their daily morning prayer meeting in these houses.

About a year or so after operations had been commenced a church, consisting of some early converts was regularly organized at the station. Accessions were afterwards made, almost every communion, say four times yearly, of converts residing in different parts of the field. These church members combined to sustain religious meetings in many neighborhoods remote from the station.

During all the eleven years, I had the honor of operating in the Hana field in the capacity of missionary, there were frequent revivals resulting in many hopeful conversions and in reforming and civilizing the masses in a marked degree. They gradually got in the way of using clothing of foreign manufacture and inhabiting better and more commodious houses; and there was developed a laudable ambition to rise out of poverty, ignorance—moral and physical degradation.

The work of the missionary was arduous, laborious, self-sacrificing and fatiguing, owing to the extent and roughness of the country to be traversed, and the hitherto untutored character of the people. It consisted in teaching school, superintending schools, preaching at home and abroad on frequent tours, dealing out school books to old and young, visiting the sick, trying to heal, at least mitigate suffering, by the use of medicine, spending weeks and weeks vaccinating all classes of all ages, as security against small pox—practising the same independently to the end, helping the people to acquire their little homesteads in fee simple, by making out the requisite papers, and serving as their correspondent, etc.; listening to their little troubles, domestic and general, and giving advice to promote harmony and good will among all; teaching the arts of civilization as well as the theory and practice of religion, laboring with wayward church members and stirring up all to more watchfulness, prayer and Christian activity—in short, utilizing all skill, ingenuity, strength, patience, etc., inherited or acquired. Indeed, I never found the day long enough for its duties, nor the night long enough to rest my body in. In nearly all these activities my excellent and sympathizing wife, participated more or less as her many family cares permitted.

For about three years consecutively, we lived in a grass house or rather two, one after the other, neither of them really impervious to rain. After occupying the first, less than a full year, it was consumed by fire, with nearly all our furniture and all our clothing, except what was attached to our persons. The fire originated from a spark blown by a.kona wind (*makani kona*) out of a small portable iron furnace placed just outside of our little kitchen built in a wrong direction from and in too close proximity to the house. As the spark touched the dwelling house in a very short space of time the whole exterior surface from bottom to top was ablaze.

I was absent at the time conducting our usual Wednesday afternoon meeting in church about one hundred rods distant, a loud cry outside was heard, my hearers rose and rushed out, I too, ran out and heard the startling cry "pau ka hale o ke kumu i ke aki." when I reach home very little could be saved besides what had already been secured, by a few near by, when the fire was first discovered, viz.: our mattrasses and bed covering, part of our library, a few chairs, table and light stand, looking glass and some crockery and glassware. But my wife's bureau full of her infant's clothing, etc., our only bedstead, my extra clothes and shoes, etc., were all consumed, leaving us almost utterly destitute. The dwelling house of Mr. and Mrs. Ives (our associates) located near by suffered the same fate, eventually, but most of their goods, also doors, windows and loose flooring were saved by the crowd while our house was being consumed. Well in the vicinity there stood a new thatched house that had never been occupied. While the devouring flames still lingered, the owner came to us and kindly offered us the use of it. He was a recent convert and had been received a church member. We gratefully accepted the favor. The people carried all that was saved from the fire into said house and spread mats upon the ground floor. We procured two rickety settees (noho loiki), placed them side by side and placed our saved mattresses and covering upon them, and thus improvised a moe oluolu. The house, 10x14 feet, was divided between our associates and us—they using two-thirds, they having all their original effects to husband, we very little of ours. Lived on common stock and sat around one table. Our cooking was done under an affair made of loose boards from Mr. Ives' ill-fated house. Soon occurred the rainy season, which greatly aggravated our pitiable condition.

That must have been a gloomy time for the two lady missionaries to spend alone, with each an infant to care for. We, their husbands, absent, hundreds of miles distant, attending general meeting at Honolulu. It was, or it seemed at the time, very important that both should be present at that session, on account of our recent losses, and we had confidence in the friendliness of the people, that they would look after and protect our families during our absence, nor were we disappointed, for on our return we found them safe and in usual health.

After enduring these straightened and destitute circumstances some months, the people built us a new thatched house, and after spending a week or two of labor upon it to make it habitable, we finally got settled, as at the beginning, before our loss. That is, we had comfortable shelters, but furniture and clothing, etc., were minus. These were replaced very gradually, from various donors and by purchase.

A second-hand bureau, without an owner, was transferred to my wife to replace hers that was lost in the fire. But its drawers were empty.. So she was necessitated to ply her faithful needle many a month to fill them. Those days preceded the invention and use of sewing machines.

As the most rigid economy was the order of the day, whatever missionaries could do, with their own hands they were expected to do, that by so much the treasury of the Board might be relieved of disbursing its precious funds. In those incipient days of the missionaries, self-sacrifice and cheap living were not only matters of conscience, but they were inculcated both by our superiors at Boston, and their subordinates at Honolulu. None thought it honorable to complain, considering that quiet submission was the wisest and safest policy.

After living three years in a grass house, we were happy to exchange it for a more permanent and agreeable structure. It was built of stone laid up in lime mortar, not, however, of the best quality. The roof, to some expense, was thatched by native workmen. I procured from Lahaina two foreign carpenters, one a Spaniard, and the other a Portuguese. After completing all the work, except that of constructing the rooms above, they insisted on leaving and returning to Lahaina —said that they could not and would not tarry any longer in so lonely and quiet a place as Hana.

I then went to work and constructed the upper apartments with my own hands, at leisure intervals. Our house finished, (the wood work inside and outside, all well painted,) appeared pleasant. We ceased not to give thanks for so comfortable a home. Our location, notwithstanding its isolation and want of cultured and congenial society, was in respect to scenery and climate, truly delightful. Ceaseless verdure met the eye in every direction, and a gentle trade wind from the northeast fanned it night and day for eight consecutive months of the year; the climate was most wholesome and agreeable.

The next enterprise of special note was the erection of a house of worship. It was built of stone and mortar. The stone was gathered from the country round about, and especially from the ruins of an old heiau. The people began by carrying the stones on their shoulders. Many were collected in this manner. But to expedite the work I borrowed a pair of oxen from Wailuku, and improvising a low truck, hitched them to it, and with this simple arrangement, all the heavy material needed was gotten on the ground. Then parties went in canoes out in the harbor, and collected coral for lime, diving for it in two and three fathoms of water. This coral they were instructed how to convert into lime. Then a dozen of our most skillful church members were furnished, each with a trowel, and taking one myself, we proceeded to lay up the walls, being waited on by a sufficient corps of mixers and hodmen. The dimensions of the building were 40 by 100 feet; the walls 14 feet high, 2½ feet thick at the foundation, and 1 foot at the top. Timber for plates, beams and rafters was obtained from the mountains. I owned a trusty, safe-footed little mule and a beautiful mare, both broken into the harness and to the saddle, the harness of my own make. These animals being equipped with harness and saddle, and placed one before the other, I mounted the mule in the rear and drove them tandem, and furnishing a party of men with axes, we all went up to the mountains by a rough and crooked path to where suitable timber was to be had. As the men prepared sticks of the required size and length, I attached my team to them and drew them down the declivity to where they could be reached by the oxen and cart. Having gotten a sufficiency of this kind of material on the ground, kind Providence sent a discharged sailor, a carpenter, to our place. Him I employed to frame the roof and raise it in position, on the walls, with the help of the people, after which a good thatch covering was applied. The women prepared mats and covered the ground floor. I myself constructed the pulpit. The natives partially seated it with settees of their own make. They had to contribute but little money towards the enterprise. They furnished all the material and nearly all the labor, and were highly gratified with their success.

A bell of several hundred pounds was procured in due time and mounted upon a round structure built of stone and mortar eighteen feet high. The people paid nearly all the expense in cash, the balance in labor.

The effort and the result were of much benefit to the church members and the people generally. They felt that they had made another step toward civilization. And it awakened in them a strong ambition to rise higher in the scale of respectability, morality and true virtue. During our occupancy of the Hana station we had three changes of associates. First, Mr. and Mrs. Ives. They remained with us several years, did good service, were excellent Christians and faithful, conscientious missionaries. But his health failed and he was necessitated to return to his friends in New England, where his wife and children soon joined him. Next were Mr. and Mrs. Rice. They were a most amiable and excellent couple. Taught and superintended the schools throughout the field. He left us, and Mr. and Mrs. Whittlesey succeeded to their place. They were agreeable and excellent friends.

After much ill health on the part of my wife, it became evident that a change of location was absolutely essential for her welfare, where congenial society could be enjoyed. An opportunity was offered to succeed Mr. Clark at Wailuku. We had occupied the Hana station eleven years, and by the good hand of the Lord, guiding us and strengthening us in all our toil, gathered a church of six hundred members and more. At Wailuku, we found a commodious dwelling house awaiting us built of stone and roofed with shingles, also a large stone house of worship, all put up in the days of Mr. Armstrong, the former Mission pastor of the station. The meeting house, however, needed repairs. It had a thatched roof of grass and a ground floor covered with dirty mats and seated with rough and rickety settees, but had a pulpit quite respectable for that age, made of nicely planed koa boards. The sides presented two tiers of windows each, of small sized glass.

The people, i. e., the church members, were soon advised to inaugurate measures to replace the old thatched roof with shingles, to floor the house with planed boards, and to seat it with respectable pews, as far as possible. They concurred and soon began the work, for there were funds of considerable amount already collected and on hand, for the purpose. Shingles were ordered from Boston, costing some thirteen dollars per thousand, including cost of freight; and other lumber needed, proportionately high. The house was fifty by one hundred feet. The rafters very steep, hence very long, presented a surface of great extent. Many thousands of shingles were required to complete the roof. One man alone (a foreigner) did the job, including the laying of the floor and seating it, as far as the amount of funds authorized. The improvement made the house much more comfortable and inviting. About three thousand dollars were expended on these repairs. My own and my wife's labors, in the Wailuku field were similar to those in my former field, and were attended with similar results.

At intervals there were religious awakenings, when many hopeful conversions occurred. More or less were received into the church at every communion.

The excitement produced by the discovery of gold in California was disastrous to religious prosperity over all the islands, especially at Wailuku. Trade of considerable magnitude with San Francisco was developed. Ships from there called often for cargoes of vegetables and other produce to supply the multitudes that were flocking into that city on their way to the gold deposits. Much money was put in circulation among the people, and because they were but partia'ly enlightened and Christianized and did not know how to utilize it properly, it did them harm, causing a prevalence of corrupting influences and thus retarded the interests of religion. It rendered the duties of the missionary more arduous. It was difficult to maintain a proper state of sentiment and practice. There was an irresistible tendency on the part of church members to become palaka and to absent themselves from meetings, and to fall into overt acts of sin and iniquity. This sad decline of religious interest was a matter of much regret and anxiety.

In 1855, occurred the death of my beloved wife, of consumption. She was not only intelligent, but affectionate and kind to her husband and her children and all, a faithful and useful assistant missionary.

The remains of mother and little daughter were buried in the church yard near to the home which we used to call our own. Their graves are side by side, and are enclosed by an iron fence. It is devoutly hoped that this area may continne to be respected and to remain intact,

The decease of my wife absolutely required my departure with the surviving children for my native land. I left in the fall of 1856, arriving at our destination in the following spring in safety and in excellent health.

I have ever since felt a lively interest in the temporal and spiritual welfare of the Hawaiian people, and do most earnestly pray that the efforts of those still laboring for their good may be crowned with great success.

LIFE AND WORK AT PUNAHOU.

BY MRS. M. S. RICE AND MISS MARCIA M. SMITH.

In the journey of life many events pass without making deep impressions. Others are living pictures fixed in the memory. Such is our removal to Punahou in the summer of 1844.

After one of those memorable schooner voyages (which, thank God, are things of the past), we reached our new home weary and sad.

In my arms a crying baby who bore the name of Emily Dole; but she whose name she had, gifted intellectually, a friend in whom I rejoiced as one that helped me, whose society would have given grace and charm to our new duties, had just been carried from Punahou to the "house appointed to all."

Many of her duties I was to assume. Was expected to be a mother to ten or twelve boys with limited wardrobes, which required two days of the week for repairs. I had also the care of their rooms. These, the boys were expected to keep in order as the school was intended to be one for manual labor. To these duties was added teaching.

Punahou, the princely gift of Father Bingham, was not as now an inviting place. It was without flowers or trees, and connected with Honolulu by a treeless plain. The adobe rooms were of the simplest construction, and an economy was necessary that forbade adornment within. Yet we had the beautiful mountains and the grand old sea to enjoy. No trees or buildings obstructed our view. Then we had the priceless spring. Its value may be inferred from the water being carried to Honolulu in demijohns, where the supply of water was from brackish wells.

All the cooking for the family was done at an open fire place with the help of a brick oven. The cook house was separated from the dining room. The path to it was without any shelter from the strong trade winds which often rushed into the house carrying things hither and thither, and we ourselves at times seemed powerless to withstand the blasts.

Perhaps we only shared the lot of those who have boarders, but our table was never satisfactory. The price paid for board was small. No fresh vegetables could be had much of the year. Until the Chinese succeeded in their gardens, it was thought impossible, except during the rainy season, to raise anything except talo, sweet potatoes and bananas. Even at that time there were many foes. The pelua, a small worm, which one year came up even to our house, was the great enemy of our vegetables. But when we did succeed was there ever such a luxury as string beans? We were associated with the Rev. Daniel Dole, an Israelite indeed, and Miss Marcia M. Smith, who still lives at an advanced age. Recently reading a letter from her, with its vigorous thought and clear handwriting, she was vividly recalled. Miss Smith would have been more popular with parents and children had she not so firmly believed in Solomon's methods. But could Punahou have survived without her wonderful self-denial, great physical strength and devotion to the interests of the school? I remember her also as the kindest of associates ever striving to carry the heavier part of the burdens.

Our first guests at Punahou were the Rev. Mr. Whitney and wife, from Kauai, he seeking relief by change from the malady for which there no cure. He was of commanding presence, a faithful and successful missionary, but most genial and sympathetic. The visit left a fragrance, especially as some remarks of his at family prayer were the means of deepening the religions impressions o one of our pupils, who is now a pillar in the Church of God.

Punahou was at that time a sort of missionary hotel, and we greatly enjoyed the visits of ou missionary friends.

Then correspondence with the parents was source of pleasure. With the Mother Lyman had an interchange of letters for nearly forty years. In one of her last letters, written in 1885, she says: "Our next meeting will be in the beyond probably, and what a meeting awaits us there. With the loved ones who have passed on before, it does not seem so far away."

Mrs. R. D. Forbes writes in 1845, expressing much sympathy in my labors, as I had then the care of all the rooms. She says, "Those long walks around the courts must be fatiguing. I could not endure them. But there is a clime where health, beauty and vigor never decay. May this glorious anticipation stimulate us to bear with meekness, patience, yea, rejoicing too, the various ills of life." Another in a loving letter writes, "It is good to walk by faith." Dear Sister Conde, she now walks by sight. The Mother Hitchcock writes in 1845, "Do be careful of your health. I often feel that dear Sister Cole shortened her days by her devotion to the dear children."

From nearly a volume of old letters I will quote no more.

From 1849 to 1852, we seemed to gain a vantage ground. Revivals were enjoyed in the school. The pupils were interested and a large proportion expressed hope in Christ. Quite a number united with the Mission Church at our General Meeting. How much those words express to us who have enjoyed these gatherings, "whither the tribes go up the tribes of the Lord" describes them. Parents and children came from the different stations with household goods sufficient to make a home in the better native houses. Then we assembled in the abobe school house, fathers, mothers, children, the older boys whittling on the back seats, mothers and daughters, with their needles. There were many opportunities of social converse. Reports were read, matters of interest discussed. Devotional services were held together; we sat down at the table of our Lord. Was there ever more soul-stirring music than our grand old hymns rolled out by the voice of Father Thurston leading in Lenox.

In 1852, there was a longer session than usual, for that year the change came. By one dash of the pen in Boston, we were changed from foreign missionaries to home missionaries, to get in part our own support, to hold property; and the property of the Board was to be divided—houses, lands and herds.

Before this, or about the same time, King Kamehameha had expressed a wish that the mission families remain here and had given to each family at a low price a small tract of land. Many of the missionaries had small patrimonies, and paid for this land. From this has arisen much scandal to the Mission, and the taunt of rich missionaries. But a careful survey of the families of the Mission will show that the majority are poor, and will convince one of the truth of a remark once made by His Excellency R. C. Wylie that the Mission had on very small salaries lived decently and raised their families creditably, not knowing of the faculty of many of the missionary mothers. That some of the children of the Mission are, compared with their parents, rich, is not strange when we consider the habits of temperance, economy and diligence in which they were trained.

During our residence at Punahou no deaths occurred, until the vacation of 1852, which was a time of tears. Charles Parsons died from over-fatigue while tramping on the mountains of Maui. He was greatly mourned, as his influence in the school was highly valued. Comely in person, gentlemanly and appreciative, he was one of the fruits of the revival, and appeared a very earnest Christian.

In August, Edward Johnson, a promising and pleasant lad of twelve years, was drowned while returning to school. The small schooner capsized, and struggling some time in the water he perished near the land.

In October, we heard of the death of Wm. Emerson. He had long been a Christian and bore the image of the Heavenly. He died at sea while voyaging for health, and his body, like that of Edward Johnson, the sea will one day give up.

In 1852, the Mission to the Caroline Islands was commenced. The noble band of missionaries were our guests. Their courage and fitness for such an enterprise seemed wonderful, and many pleasant hours we enjoyed in their society. Said a gentleman who had been at the southern islands, "They cannot live there, and you will soon see what is left of them back again." But the mission continues to the present time.

In 1853, were the terrible ravages of the small pox. There was a large temporary hospital east of Punahou, and the yellow flag everywhere floating, saddened and depressed. The school did not commence until the pestilence had passed, so that my husband was able to devote his whole time to the sufferers in the homes and hospitals.

Shall I withold the tribute to the memory of the just man whose tender, loving sympathy enabled me to endure the ten years at Punahou. He was not only devoted to the school, but could never forget the Hawaiians whom he loved, and for whom he labored even after failing health prevented his efforts for Punahou. As was said of him, "His life sprung from a deep inner sympathy with God's will, and was therefore all that was true, beautiful and right."

I must also mention the second wife of Mr. Dole, the loving and devoted stepmother, our associate, not only at Punahou, but afterward on Kauai.

In the spring of 1854, we left Punahou poor and warn, feeling that our salary was of more value to the school than our services. The recompense has not been witheld. That the school continues prosperous and useful is a comfort indeed. Another comfort is the characters and usefulness of our pupils, though by no means claiming that "our boys" owe all to us. We did not spoil them; but did, with imperfection, it is true, but honestly and earnestly, toil for them.

When last in the States-a gentleman said to me, "Gen. Armstrong, from your islands, is one of the most useful men in the country." I felt a glow of happiness as I remembered him in my care so taxing my patience in many ways, once by his continued and loud crying at the smallest annoyance.

Then many of our boys are classed with those whose "beatiful feet have brought glad tidings," and I am sure those feet have been covered with many a thread from my needle.

Alhough in 1882, losing such dear and valued pupils, the best did not all die. Two who were perfection in deportment and scholarship are still living, honored and useful. Then from among those early pupils I find now my dearest friends, with whom I take "sweet counsel." Lovers of Hawaii are they, and laborers for the church in in her borders. The difference of age only increases our tender interest in each other.

Though it was often very hard at Punahou, with perplexing questions and conscious mistakes, as I review our lifework I must be thankful for ten years' service at Punahou.

―――――o―――――

MEMORIES OF PUNAHOU,

BY MARCIA M. SMITH.

A quiet rumor has come to me over the great waters and across the continent, of a notable gathering *to be*, on the sunny islands of the sea. The only way in which I can be present at that gathering is by a kindly greeting through the medium of the pen.

Both the occasion and the place turn my thoughts back to a period *more* than fifty years ago, when the incipient desire was awakened, to be one among those who should carry the news of salvation to the ignorant and dark hearted.

How that desire was nurtured by the Spirit and the Grace of God ; how His Providence led me by a way that I did not choose for myself, till my feet stood on the deck of the Mary Frazier, bound to the Sandwich Islands, as one of that company whose arrival you commemorate to-day. On the 12th of February, 1837, we were off Cape Horn, probably three or four miles from land. Under the genial influence of sun and breeze like that of a bright April day in the land of their birth, that company gathered on the deck to worship God, in services appropriate to the Holy Sabbath. Two months later, she anchored in the harbor of Honolulu. That was also the Holy Sabbath.

Who can analyze the sensations of that hour, as they were molded by the peculiar character of each individual of that company, as they first looked on the land they had voluntarily chosen for their future home? We will not here attempt it. Gratitude and praise for the many and peculiar mercies of the voyage, filled every soul, inciting to a new consecration of heart and life, to the work their Father had appointed to each.

To me, it was a "red letter day," whose memory can never fade, or pass away. It was as a mold for the future of my life.

The next June found each one with his location and work assigned him, for the present, by the united wisdom of the Mission Band, assembled at their annual meeting. They had only to accept, and with cheerful hearts and willing hands engage in the work allotted to each.

I went as teacher, pro tem., for the children of the missionaries, to commence the work at Honolulu station, until other plans could be devised and executed.

There I labored as best I could five years, excepting one year on Kauai.

In 1841, buildings were erected at Punahou, for a boarding school for the children of the mission families. Then and there, by the united wisdom of those veterans in the field, men and women, to be nourished by their prayers and tears, was laid the foundation of what you now rejoice in as *Oahu College*. In 1842, Rev. Daniel Dole and lady were appointed to commence and take charge of a boarding school at Punahou.

An assistant being needed for the care of the domestic department, I was requested to assume its duties, as my health did not allow me to teach. To this I assented conditionally. Of the five associates with whom I labored for ten years, only one remains to testify to the ceaseless toil, and anxious care, that guarded by day and night, the physical, mental and moral development of these youths, taken as it were from their mothers' arms, and with many anxious thoughts, with weeping and prayers given to our care, to train for God and the world. In this effort we shared mutually, hopefully, and confidingly, and rejoiced together in the success that attended and followed our united labors.

Called by the Providence of God, to leave that cherished work, for the care of an aged and infirm mother, till the river lay between us; and since that time filling my appointed place as God has given me strength, in the care of the aged and feeble until they too, left me one by one, and passed to the other side.

Through all this, the memory of Punahou has not become dimmed, or the remembrance of those who were fellow voyagers across the waste of waters, till we found that bright spot in the Pacific. The one so changed as not to be recognizable; the others not forgotten, but followed, one after another, to their long rest from toil; till there remain of the thirty-two who composed that company, only eleven, and only six with you. Surely we should burnish our weapons of warfare, and fill up the measure left to us, knowing that the day is at hand, when we can no longer labor to turn souls from darkness to light, or lead them to the Cross of Christ. And let those among you, who stand in the place of the fallen, see to it, that they honor the God of their fathers, by striving to save the ignorant and degraded about them.

Many kindly greetings and prayers will be wafted to you on that memorable day, that it may be a season of joy and gladness, despite the tender memories that cluster around your hearts. God grant, that you may each be made better, as well as happier, by its genial and far reaching influence.

Ever one with you in spirit and in loving service of our Lord and Master.

ABOUT THE MARQUESAS, AND THE LITTLE I KNOW OF EVENTS THAT TRANSPIRED THERE FIFTY YEARS AGO.

BY MARY E. PARKER.

In the winter of 1827, I was in New York, and went one evening to Wall-St. Church to hear the Rev. Charles Stewart lecture on Missions in the Pacific. He had been a missionary of the A. B. C. F. M. to the Hawaiian Isles; been to the Marquesas Isles; saw the finest race of aborigines, and they were the most numerous. The former was a fact. The last item, an utter mistake, as we found them in 1833.

Without romance, I thought then it would be well to go there and teach such a people lessons in civilization and religion as Mr. Stewart said, they had neither. The thought was transient, but not wholly lost, and came up again, to be settled in Hawaii at a meeting of the missionaries of the American Board in Lahaina. Mr. Parker and myself there had our appointment from the General Meeting of the Mission. Mr. and Mrs. Armstrong, and Mr. and Mrs. Alexander had theirs from the Board at Boston to go to the Marquesas.

We three families made the number designated by the Boston Board. At Honolulu, dear Mrs. Bingham, a most loving, disinterested friend, fitted me out with her well-trained servant, saying she could do without him better than I could in the dark land, to which we were going.

She knew better than I, then; knew what the

words "heathen darkness" meant. Let me here say, on my return to Hawaii, she sent for me to come to her sick bed, mingled her tears with mine, and said, "*Don't be discouraged.*"

Mr. and Mrs. Armstrong, Mr. and Mrs. Alexander had been one year in Hawaii, and in measure were prepared by a knowledge of Hawaii's customs and language to go to this field and labor among a people, similar in language, having affinities in other directions. They had books to take along—besides, they had two small children to take along, to cheer the future!

They had, each family, a trusty, trusted Hawaiian. But for these Hawaiians—three—who went with us, we must have suffered extremely with hunger, so it looks, for weeks we could not venture out doors to cook our bread fruit or boil our water on the stones, because of the crowds that surrounded our dwelling place.

Suffice, in August, 1833, we three families embarked on the "Dhaulie," Capt. Bancroft, for the Marquesas, by way of Tahiti. Were received kindly and entertained hospitably by the English missionaries a week and more. And Mr. Bicknell, the father of Brother Bicknell, put on board for us a cow, giving milk. This, it was thought, saved the lives of the children; of one of them certainly, Sister Armstrong's little girl one year old, and delicate. And the cow served us nobly, the eight months there, and was the only luxury we knew by way of food.

We must have reached the Nukuhua Bay, called Washington Bay also, sometime in August. Dates escape me as they did after we left Hawaii, till our return here; life was one episode, something thrown into life and still an unsolved problem, when I think of all that befell us, and our mission as wisely ordered, no doubt it was.

Capt. Bancroft had his orders to stop one week with his vessel. If we found it unsafe to land, and remain, he was to return us to Hawaii. The savages—for they were that—came around the vessel in great numbers. Some came on board; no women came. The captain said he was to take us back—his opinion. But we had come to stay. Christ said there were two persons to whom all things were possible. "All things are possible with God, and all things are possible to him that believeth." We belong to the class of believers, and made preparation to go on shore. The first day, I think, from arrival, we landed our effects. The brethren from the first had been on shore providing our homes. We women, with the children, were the first white women and children ever seen by the natives of Nuhioa. On our walk of a half a mile or so, the women would follow us in crowds, some running before, some at our side, exclaiming, "motaki," good; coming close and lifting our bonnets for a fuller view. A long shed, the best in the Bay, was given us for a temporary home. The ridge pole, twenty or thirty or more feet, and from it was thatch, enclosing tight that side. Eaves descended to within four feet on the other side of the stone pavement, which was the floor and verandah of the building. This space is left open in all their homes, for ingress and light. Ours had been boarded up with rough boards from the vessel, and three small doors made for our convenience, or necessity rather; no other entrance left to the building, and those doors were kept closed after we had entered. In one end of this shed was our general storeroom, ten feet; next came my room, twelve feet; next, Mrs. Alexander's, same dimensions; then Mrs. Armstrong's on the end. She had the benefit of a roaring surf, day and night, as the building was nigh the water. Our partitions were curtains, or furniture, as most convenient, shutting out sight but not sound; and we could speak to each other, and were one family, only that neither room had space for a table around which we could all gather. I think we tried it only once. While living in this building we felt secure. Hape, who owned it, was our protector, for though there was no government there, and the people all lawless, he was so much revered that any tabu of his was sacredly kept. This we found out by nothing of ours being taken; not even a tin cup, though left out doors under his care, on our arrival.

The only scare we knew while living in this primitive way, was when Mr. Alexander and Mr. Parker went to visit the Tapi valley, that took them from home one night. To prevent loneliness, Mrs. Alexander said, "Come to my room and sleep." In the night we were awakened by horrible yells, and the sound came nearer and nearer till we held our breath with fear. We could not flee, and what was to be done with Willie, the baby? Would he wake and make the exposure great for him? We could only look upward, and keep quiet, when the sounds, after coming nearer began to recede, we knew we were safe from attack. In the morning, we ascertained that the fishermen had taken a shark, and this demonstration celebrated the event.

The brethren held meetings under the shade trees (beautiful foliage from the mountain peaks to the shore). The women and men came in not great numbers; brought their work, the women their braid, the men their tools; quite an industrious people, knowing no particular day of rest. But they were listeners, and had their replies. Sometimes it was emphatic—"That's a lie." Could not easily be taught a creed one might imagine. How then reach them? By kindness? They had no needs! A singular people. Had no brawls among themselves; no quarreling among children; no love for others; none for themselves, only "hate" for their foes, and this alone showed they had souls. They would fight. It was their pastime to kill and eat their prisoners taken in war. This they did, kill and eat, while close by us.

We built our homes, placing them close together, so we might speak to each other from our doors. It was a difficult tug to get them up, but very comfortable homes they were, with doors and no windows, no floors.

Then Hape died and was hung in the trees, on the tabu heiau, that no one of us ventured on except Mrs. Armstrong. The natives said she would die, their opinion if she ventured. She did not, and their opinion was like many others they had formed, false. They saw it.

But Hape was fed daily, and soon he became a nuisance to all about the place, and to us in particular, no help for it except when the wind favored us, as it sometimes did, blowing in another direction. I think we did love Hape, but he was an exception to his race, as was one woman, very friendly.

Mr. Osmond, missionary from Society Islands, visited us. This proved to be the turning point in our mission. He gave the brethren much information that led eventually to the disbanding of the mission. We all knew the American Board would order it done, so soon as they were made acquainted with the circumstances. To wait and hear from them would take time, years possibly, and great expense must go on in that time. We could not live there as we were living, and do anything for the natives of any permanence.

Two whaleships came in with their friendly captains. The "Benjamin Bush," Capt. Coffin, would take us to Honolulu with our trunks of clothing. The other ship would take our books and what we had worth taking to Tahiti, whence we might some time get them. The sailors from both ships come on shore and formed a line of protection for us mothers to the beach, where boats awaited us to take us to the ship. It was not the mothers that had anything to fear, except for our children, four in number. These they would have taken possession of had it been possible. It had been attempted, Mrs. Armstrong thought, in regard to her little daughter—a fascinating child and not afraid of the natives—that they wanted to take, and often asked for. My six weeks old baby I wrapped closely in my apron, and brought him safely to Hawaii, glad myself to come.

After hearing from the American Board that they approved of our wisdom in disbanding the mission, we were received into favor here.

---o---

SUPPLEMENTARY NOTE TO STATISTICAL TABLE ON PAGES 128-37.

By a letter lately (June 28th) received, from the Rev. T. Dwight Hunt, more accurate information has been obtained concerning his descendants. This came too late, however, for insertion in its place in the statistical table on pages 128–37.

Only four of the children born to Mr. Hunt were recorded there. He has had twelve, eight of whom are now living, and eleven grandchildren. This then adds nineteen to the sum total of descendants enumerated in the table.

Mrs. Mary H. Hunt died in 1861, instead of 1857, as recorded in the table.

Mr. Hunt was married again in 1862 to Miss Mary E. Preston, who died in 1863, of diptheria.

He married for his third wife, Miss Sarah O. Nash, at Marshall, Michigan. Mr. Hunt writes from Chile, Monroe Co., N. Y., where he is settled over a parish near Rochester, his native city.

A letter from Rev. D. T. Conde, in answer to enquiries, states that he married for his second wife, Mrs. Hannah Williams (Rice), of Cooperstown, N. Y. This information, also, came too late for insertion in the table.

Undoubtedly the statistics in the table are in many instances incorrect and incomplete. If those who recognize any errors in names, dates, places, or in data as to descendants, will be so kind as to send notice of such errors to the Corresponding Secretary of the Hawaiian Mission Children's Society, at Honolulu, it will confer a great favor upon those who have labored to compile the historical table, and who still wish to render it as complete as possible for the benefit of those who may be called upon to do a similar work in the future.

www.ingramcontent.com/pod-product-compliance
Lightning Source LLC
LaVergne TN
LVHW051555070426
835507LV00021B/2586